RUSSIA CHANGES: THE EVENTS OF AUGUST 1991 AND THE RUSSIAN CONSTITUTION

RUSSIA CHANGES: THE EVENTS OF AUGUST 1991 AND THE RUSSIAN CONSTITUTION

Edited by A.S. Durgo

Nova Science Publishers, Inc.

Nova Science Publishers, Inc.
6080 Jericho Turnpike, Suite 207
Commack, New York 11725

Book Production Manager: Denise Engelhardt
Cover Design: Elenor Kallberg

Library of Congress Cataloguing-in-Publication Data available upon request

ISBN 0-56072-079-4

Printed in the United States of America

CONTENTS

PART I
EVENTS OF AUGUST 18–21, 1991

THE METAMORPHOSIS BEGINS

PART II

PART I

EVENTS OF AUGUST 18–21, 1991

AUGUST 1991: HOW NOT TO STAGE A COUP D'ETAT

By Maxim Sokolov and Leonid Skoptsov

The putsch which started on the night of August 18 had turned into a ridiculous parody of a coup d'etat by the morning of August 21. The putschists once again confirmed the validity of the "first commandment of a traitor:" a conspiracy either succeeds in the first three hours or does not succeed at all.

Apoplectic Snuff-Box

In their first appeal the putschists made no secret of their allegiance to the ideals of the Great Empire, and, in all probability, this was the root cause of their failure. There is the impression that the pledges about the "Unity of the Fatherland" were not simple demagogy (which is certainly necessary in any putsch) but reflected the plotters' sincere belief that the integral Empire exists in reality, not only in their feverish imaginations. For this reason, they followed the standard recipe of palace revolutions: they strike the Emperor on the head with a snuff-box and sorrowfully inform the people that the Emperor was struck by an apoplectic fit. Then the authors of the apoplectic fit divide the loot. No one judges the victors' actions because there is no one to judge: the dead do not bite, while the subjects, awakening in the morning, learn that historical justice has triumphed once again.

The flourishing of humanism, characteristic of the 20th century, has changed the classical pattern just a little: the victims of a coup are sometimes given the opportunity to go abroad to have a rest (the Latin American variant) or to the dacha (the variant of Khrushchev, Malenkov or Molotov).

To all appearances, it was their faith in the effectiveness of the classical patterns that caused the putschists to make a gross mistake: having successfully isolated Gorbachev in his Crimean estate and broadcast an array of reports and appeals through the seized channels of the State Committee for Television and Radio Broadcasting, they rested on their laurels right away. The Russian leaders, who could have easily been eliminated on the morning of August 19 by a platoon of soldiers, remained in place, the House of the Government of the RSFSR was not captured, and Yeltsin was given the extra time he needed.

It looks like the conspirators, who cannot think in any other way but within centralist categories, sincerely believed that the removal of Gorbachev resolved all problems. But such a simple and convenient method can be effective only in a genuine Empire. What Robespierre called the "hydra of federalism"—as a result of the decentralization of the state, a new head grows instead of the cut-off one—is an important political factor in such a state formation as the present-day Soviet Union. Instead of the cut-off head of Mikhail Gorbachev the putschists saw the head of Boris Yeltsin which was even more unpleasant to them: for some unknown reason, "dissenter" Yeltsin got the chance to reach the White House without hindrance, to quell the panic in the ranks of his supporters, and to start organizing the Resistance.

Chaos as the Best Means of Defending the Constitution

It was noted long ago that Yeltsin acts best in extreme situations. This held true in this instance, as well: from 11:00 of August 19 he began to act following the principle: "forging one decree after another like horse-shoes, hitting some on the forehead, others in the nose, still others in the groin, and some in the eye." The essence of the hosts of decrees boiled down to the following:

—the members of the State Emergency Committee are especially dangerous state criminals (the Russian lawyers determined the activities of the State Emergency Committee as falling within Article 64, "High Treason," of the Criminal Code of the Russian Federation, which envisages capital punishment);

—execution of the orders of the State Emergency Committee by Russia's officials shall also be qualified as a crime against the state;

—in the absence of the legitimate President of the USSR Yeltsin assumes all his constitutional duties to suppress treason.

Naturally, not all officials immediately began to fulfill Yeltsin's orders; on the whole, they preferred not to fulfill any directions whatsoever, and absolute chaos reigned supreme across Russia. Everyone was guided by the principle "all at sixes and sevens." For instance, part of the Taman division went over to Russia, part sided with the Emergency Committee, but the largest part "sided with itself" and preferred to bide its time.

This was precisely what Yeltsin needed. He was accustomed to the non-fulfillment of his orders, and there was nothing new in this for everyone. But if a putsch, the essence of which is to "establish order with an iron hand," does not result in iron order but in absolute chaos the traitors' undertaking looses all attractiveness in the public's eyes. The public at large arrives at the conclusion that chaos without tanks is certainly more preferable than chaos with tanks. Using the language of law, this means that the ideas of a constitutional system attract people again.

What's Behind the Mask?

The hesitation of the Emergency Committee leads to the conclusion that at first officials, primarily, to all appearances, Baklanov and Kryuchkov and maybe Pugo (Yazov was the second echelon; if Gorbachev had not been isolated, he would not have dared to involve the Army in a conflict with the Russian population, people who know him say), but not the Union power structures headed by them were the motive forces of the coup. This alone can explain the sluggishness (inexcusable for the Marxists--Leninists), the absence of tough repressions and the continuous attempts to rely on Soviet law.

By the night of August 20 to 21 it became clear that the members of the Emergency Committee worried mainly over ways to avoid the criminal sanctions envisaged by Article 64 of the Criminal Code of the RSFSR. Yanayev was "hesitating and groaning," Yazov either resigned or allowed the rumors about his resignation to be spread, and the others were keeping mum. Unexpectedly, all of them proved to be open for contacts: Gennady Burbulis called them up several times during the night. It was not clear any longer who was giving orders on the troops' movements.

And the last stage---the escape of the members of the Emergency Committee---not only turned them into a kind of punishment battalion but also dramatically changed the position of the figures who "did not have a finger in the pie"---Pugo's Deputy Boris Gromov, Chief of the General Staff Mikhail Moiseyev and to a certain extent even Anatoly Lukyanov (despite the Russian leadership's intention to thoroughly investigate his role in the putsch). Common to all of them is that "they had just returned from leave and did not know anything;" that in the present situation they have remained unblemished, and that in the process of the return to normal life it is quite enough for them to make statements to the effect that THEY will never permit anything of the kind and to occupy the posts which have so fortunately become vacant.

THE HOUR OF GRAVE DANGER: BORIS YELTSIN ADDRESSES THE NATION

At this tense moment I turn to you my fellow countrymen. A handful of political adventurists have proclaimed themselves the supreme authority. They have created an anti-constitutional conspiracy and have thereby committed the gravest crime against the state. The democratic changes our people struggled for over the past five years have been trampled underfoot. In just one night freedom of speech, street processions and demonstrations and the legitimate right of citizens to express their views and uphold their stance have been eliminated. All means of communication have been concentrated in the hands of the putschists. The legally elected representatives of the peoples of Russia have been given no chance to address the electorate.

Using the traditional demagoguery, which has been tried and tested over the years, the putschists blame all our current difficulties on the democrats and promise economic recovery and a better life, security and prosperity for the citizens of the USSR. What a hypocritical lie!

Surely Pavlov is responsible for rocketing inflation and unprecedented price rises this year?

Surely Yazov as leader of the most corrupt highest placed generals, is responsible for the poverty and lawlessness of our servicemen?

Surely Pugo bears personal responsibility for the blood shed in the Baltic republics?

Surely Starodubtsev, leader of the organization of Soviet land-owners is to blame, owing to the stance he assumed, for the abortive collection of last year's bumper crops?

And these are the people who promise to "restore order in the country!"

Their criminal deeds have left the country on the brink of terror and transformed them into petty criminals. The "order" which these latter-day "saviors" promise us would be the rule of an iron fist—suppression of dissidents, concentration camps and arrests made in the dark of the night.

All this can arouse only one feeling in all normal people—contempt. What can be more absurd than an illegally formed committee demanding the disbandment of legally elected bodies of state power? This constitutes a glaring disrespect for the Constitution of the USSR and the Constitution of Russia. It is a crime which will receive inevitable, just retribution from the people. Each will get what he deserves.

The leadership of Russia has taken resolute steps to cut short the activities of the self-styled committee in the republic.

Following a decree of the President of the Russian Federation, its activities are classified as illegal and its decrees null and void throughout Russia. All the executive bodies of the USSR, including the KGB, the Interior Ministry and the Defense Ministry, which function in the Russian Federation, are re-subordinated directly to the people-elected President of Russia. The actions of officials fulfilling the decisions of this committee are punishable under the Criminal Code of the Russian Federation. Colonel-General Kobets has been appointed Chairman of the State Committee of the Russian Federation for Defense.

An interim committee for the management of the republic's national economy has been formed. Appealing to the citizens of Russia on August 19 the leaders of the Russian Federation urged them to support the legitimately elected bodies of power and adopt different forms of civil protest in order to stop the activities of the impostors.

Following a meeting of the Presidium of the Supreme Soviet of the Russian Federation, held on August 19, it was decided that an emergency session of the Supreme Soviet be convened on August 21.

Citizens of Russia, just remember everything Yanayev, the self-proclaimed "President of the USSR," said and did over the past 24 hours. His main goal is to isolate Russia from the other republics of the USSR.

The putschists have promised "preferential treatment" to the Ukraine, Kazakhstan, Uzbekistan and Armenia throughout the emergency situation. The dictatorship has raised its heavy boot-clad foot to strike at Russia. Russia is the prime target of this conspiracy.

The coup was accomplished on August 19. It is perfectly clear that this date was not chosen at random: it was the day before the signing of a new Union Treaty. Despite all the compromises made, this Treaty was to put an end to the omnipotent power of the CPSU and the military-industrial complex.

Listening to the comments of those who masterminded this putsch, I am appalled at their degree of moral degradation. Yesterday the leadership of Russia was criticized for its apparent reluctance to sign a Union Treaty. Today, people are told that our desire to sign it is merely an attempt to counter the renewal of the Union.

The new Union Treaty would objectively deprive each organizer of this putsch of his post. Herein lies the secret grounds behind this conspiracy and the prime motivation for the actions of its culprits. Their profuse talk on the destiny of the Motherland is no more than a pretext for their own greedy ambitions.

I did not mention the CPSU by mere chance. Let us face it---this party was in fact "the organizing and inspiring force" of the putsch. Isn't it true that the Committee disbanded through its decrees, all parties excluding the Communist Party and banned all the newspapers except the Communist ones? I am convinced that the time will come when the leaders of the CPSU will swear that they had nothing to do with this crime against the people. But they will hardly be able to camouflage with demagoguery the essence of their activities---the struggle against the people in order to protect their own privileges.

I want to state once again most resolutely that all the events of the past 24 hours are symptomatic of a coup and nothing else. Its leaders are state criminals. That is why the fulfillment of their decisions by Russian officials will be considered as a crime under the Criminal Code of the Russian Federation and so they will be punished in keeping with the law.

In this hour of deadly danger I appeal to you, the people of Russia, to support the very people you elected and entrusted with the fate of Russia. The people of Russia should unite together and confront the reaction as one body. We should oppose the tanks and armored personnel carriers with a common will and desire to prevent a dictatorship. Unity and solidarity are the key forces behind our victory.

My appeal is to the citizens of Russia who represent all ethnic communities. Forget your ethnic differences. If Russia is free we will be able to solve all our problems---without any violence, loss of blood or humiliation of anyone. We will not attempt to "bewitch" the ailments of our society. We will cure them. We know the recipe---mutual respect and accord.

I once again appeal to you, Russian soldiers and officers. Do not let yourselves be turned into a blind weapon guarding the privileges and prosperity of a handful of hypocrites who have lost all sense of moderation. I hope that in this tragic hour you will be able to distinguish between the truth and vile lies.

I believe that the honor and glory of the Russian army will not be stained with the blood of its own people.

A throne can be built with bayonets. But can it last? I am sure that there is no return to the past. The days of the plotters are numbered. Law and constitutional order will prevail. Russia will be free.

Boris Yeltsin
President of the Russian Federation

August 20, 1991

DECREES, STATEMENTS AND COMMUNIQUES OF THE PRESIDENT OF THE RUSSIAN SOVIET FEDERATED SOCIALIST REPUBLIC AND OTHER LEADERS

Decree
By the President of the Russian Soviet

Taking into account the present situation, I hereby resolve that:

O.I. Lobov, First Vice-Chairman of the RSFSR Council of Ministers, A.V. Yablokov, member of the RSFSR State Council, and S.N. Krasavchenko, member of the Presidium of the RSFSR Supreme Soviet, shall organize the management of the national-economic complex of the Republic and, if necessary, secure the efficiency of the operation of major state structures.

I authorize, for carrying out the objective set, the enlistment of necessary officials on behalf of the President of the RSFSR.

All organizations located on the territory of the RSFSR shall render necessary assistance.

President of the RSFSR B. Yeltsin

The Kremlin, Moscow,
August 19, 1991
No. 62

Decree
By the President of the Russian Soveit Federative Socialist Republic

In connection with the actions of a group of persons who have declared themselves the State Committee for the State of Emergency, I hereby resolve:

1. To consider the declaration of the Committee unconstitutional and qualify the actions of its organizers as a coup d'etat which is nothing other than a state crime.
2. All the decisions taken on behalf of the so-called committee for the state of emergency shall be deemed unlawful and having no force on the territory of the RSFSR. On the territory of the Russian Federation there shall operate the lawfully-elected authority in the person of the President, Supreme Soviet and Chairman of the Council of Ministers, of all state and local bodies of power and administration of the RSFSR.
3. Actions by officials carrying out the decisions of the said committee shall be subject to the RSFSR Penal Code and prosecution under the law.

This Decree shall enter into force upon its signature.

President of the RSFSR B. Yeltsin

The Kremlin, Moscow,
August 19, 1991
No. 59

ROSSIYA

Newspaper of the Presidium of the Supreme Soviet
Of the Russian Federation

Special Issue

TO THE CITIZENS OF RUSSIA

On the night of August 18, the legally elected President was removed from power.

Whatever the motives to justify this removal from power may be, we are confronted with a right-wing, reactionary and anti-constitutional coup.

For all the difficulties which have befallen the people, the democratic process is broadening and becoming irreversible. The peoples of Russia are becoming the masters of their own future. The uncontrollable rights of unconstitutional bodies, including party ones, have been considerably curbed. The leaders of the Russian Federation have assumed a resolute position in relation to the Union Treaty, aspiring for the strength of the Soviet Union and the unity of Russia. Our position on this score made it possible to accelerate the drafting of the Union Treaty, coordinate it with all the union republics and fix the data for its signing---August 20.

Such a course of events has angered the reactionary forces, pushing them to irresponsible and adventurist attempts to settle the most complicated political and economic problems by force. Earlier, attempts had already been made to accomplish a coup.

We did and do believe that methods of force are inadmissible. They discredit the USSR in the eyes of the world, undermine our prestige in the world community and are hurling us back to the epoch of cold war and isolation of the Soviet Union from the world community.

All this forces us to declare the so-called committee which has come to power, illegal. Aware of our responsibility, we declare all of the decisions and instructions of the so-called committee to be illegal.

We are convinced that the local bodies of power will strictly observe the constitutional Laws and Decrees of the President of the Russian Federation.

We urge all citizens of Russia to give adequate rebuff to the putschists, and demand that the country be put back on the road of normal constitutional development.

Undoubtedly, conditions must be created allowing President Gorbachev to speak to the nation. We demand immediate convocation of an extraordinary congress of People's Deputies of the USSR.

We are convinced that our compatriots will not allow the tyranny and lawlessness of the brazen putschists to assert themselves. We urge servicemen to display their sense of civic duty and not to take part in the reactionary coup.

Pending the implementation of these demands, we urge all to go on an indefinite strike.

We do not doubt that the world community will objectively assess this cynical attempt to carry out a right-wing coup.

President of the Russian Federation Boris Yeltsin

Chairman of the Council of Ministers
of the Russian Federation Ivan Silayev

Acting Chairman of the Supreme Soviet
of the Russian Federation Ruslan Khasbulatov

August 19, 1991. 9 a.m.

Decree
By the President of the Russian Soviet Federative Socialist Republic

In connection with the steps made by a group of people who have called themselves the State Committee for the State of Emergency I hereby resolve:

1. To consider the institution of the Committee unconstitutional and qualify the actions of its organizers as a state coup which is nothing but a state crime.

2. To consider all the resolutions passed on behalf of the so-called state of emergency committee illegal and invalid in the Russian Federation. The territory of the Russian Federation shall be governed by the legitimate bodies of power in the person of the President, the Supreme Soviet and the Chairman of the Council of Ministers, and by all of the state and local bodies of power and administration of the Russian Federation.

3. The actions of the officials implementing the resolutions of the above-mentioned committee shall come under the criminal code of the Russian Federation and be prosecuted by the law.

The present Decree shall go into effect the moment it is signed.

President of the Russian Federation Boris Yeltsin

Moscow, Kremlin
August 19, 1991
No. 59

Decree
By the President of the Russian Soviet Federative Socialist Republic

In view of the current situation I hereby resolve:

To charge First Deputy-Chairman of the Council of Ministers of the Russian Federation, O. Lobov, Member of the State Council of the Russian Federation, A. Yablokov, and Member of the Presidium of the Supreme Soviet of the Russian Federation S. Krasavchenko with the mission of ensuring emergency control over the Republic's economic complex and, if necessary, efficient work of the main state structures.

On behalf of the President of the Russian Federation to involve the required executives in this work in order to fulfill this task.

All organizations located on the territory of the Russian Federation shall be rendered them necessary assistance.

President of the Russian Federation Boris Yeltsin

Moscow, Kremlin
August 19, 1991
No. 62.

PRESIDENT

of the Russian Soviet Federative Socialist Republic

DECREE

Having accomplished a state coup and forcibly removed from power the Soviet President who is the Supreme commander of the USSR Armed Forces,

USSR Vice-President G. Yanayev,

USSR Prime Minister V. Pavlov,

Chairman of the KGB V. Kryuchkov,

USSR Minister of Internal Affairs B. Pugo,

USSR Defense Minister D. Yazov,

Chairman of the Peasants' Union V. Starodubtsev,

First Deputy Chairman of the State Committee for Defense O. Baklanov,

President of the Association of Industry, Construction and Communication A. Tizyakov

and their accomplices have committed grave state crimes, having violated Article 62 of the USSR Constitution, articles 64, 69, 70, 70 (1) and 72 of the Criminal Code of the Russian Federation and corresponding articles of the criminal codes of the USSR and of the Union republics.

Having betrayed the nation, the Motherland and the Constitution, they have put themselves above the law.

On the basis of the above-mentioned facts I hereby resolve that:

The citizens working in the bodies of the procurator's office, state security and internal affairs of the USSR and the Russian Federation, and servicemen who are aware of their responsibility for the future of the nation and the state, and who resent dictatorship, civil war and bloodshed shall be given the right to act in accordance with the Constitution and the laws of the USSR and the Russian Federation. As President of Russia, on behalf of the people who have elected me, I guarantee legal protection and moral support to you.

The future of Russia and the Union is in your hands.

President of the Russian Federation Boris Yeltsin
Moscow, Kremlin
August 19, 1991
No. 63

To His Holiness
The Holy Patriarch of Moscow
and all Russia
Alexiy II

Your Holiness,

The tragic events which have occurred last night impel me to appeal to You and through You to all believers of Russia.

An act of brazen lawlessness has taken place. A group of high-ranking corrupt party bureaucrats has accomplished an anti-constitutional state coup. The legitimately elected president of the USSR has been removed from power. In fact, a state of emergency has been introduced on the entire territory of the USSR, which has trampled underfoot the Constitution and laws of the USSR, as well as the constitution and laws of the sovereign republics of the Union.

Indicatively, all this has happened on the eve of the conclusion of the Union treaty, which would open real prospects for overcoming the crisis, for attaining freedom and embarking on the road of democracy and progress.

The coup has trampled underfoot not only our state system and growing democracy. It has trampled underfoot our civic choice. The clouds of lawlessness and tyranny have gathered over the country again.

In this tragic hour, I urge You to use Your authority among the religious confessions and believers, as well as the influence of the Church in our society, and not to stay on the sidelines of the events, as they are directly connected with the vocation to which You, Your Holiness, have devoted your life---service for the benefit of the people and concern for their hearts and souls. Having suffered a great deal during the years of totalitarianism, the Church may once again become a victim of tyranny and lawlessness.

The believers, all Russian people and the whole of Russia are waiting for Your word.

Boris Yeltsin
August 19, 1991

Statement

An extraordinary event has occurred in the life of our country. President of the USSR, Mikhail Gorbachev, elected by the Congress of People's Deputies of the Soviet Union, was left outside supreme power.

The circumstances of this remain unclear.

Such a situation confuses the minds of millions of our compatriots who question the legality of the newly set-up State of Emergency Committee, which has announced that it has assumed supreme power in the USSR.

In view of this, we state that we need to hear the voice of President Gorbachev and know his attitude to the events.

We hope that the Supreme Soviet of the USSR will give an objective assessment of the events and take resolute measures to stabilize the situation in the country.

We appeal to all children of the Russian Orthodox Church, to all our people and, above all, to our army, to show self-control in this critical moment in the life of our Fatherland and to prevent bloodshed.

We pray zealously to God and urge all children of our Church to do the same. May He send down peace upon our country so they can continue to tend their home in accordance with their free choice and the generally-accepted ethical and legal norms.

Patriarch of Moscow and All Russia

August 20

APPEAL

by the Patriarch of Moscow and All Russia Alexiy II to Compatriots

Brothers and sisters,

The fragile civil peace in our society has been broken. Reports are coming which say that an open armed clash and bloodshed are beginning. In such a situation, it is my duty as Patriarch to warn all those who cherish the word of the Church and who are not indifferent to it: all those who are raising arms against their neighbors and unarmed people are committing a grave sin which alienates them from the Church and from God. Such people deserve more tears and prayers than their victims. May God rid us of the awful sin of fratricide. Hence I warn all my compatriots:

The Church does not and cannot bless illegal and violent actions which may cause bloodshed.

I urge all of you, dear ones, to do everything you can to disallow the flame of tribal war from flaring up among you. Stop!

I beg the soldiers and their commanders to recall that no one can fix or pay the price of human life.

I beg the Holy Virgin, the patroness of our city, not to deprive us of Her protection in these days of the Assumption Fast and to save all of us. Mother of God, help us to reconcile with each other, with the truth and with God!

Alexiy II, Patriarch of Moscow and All Russia

August 21, 1991. 1:30

To Chairman of the
Supreme Soviet of the USSR
A. Lukyanov

In view of the unconstitutional actions of a group of people who call themselves "the Soviet leadership," we find it necessary to urgently take the following measures:

1. To organize, within 24 hours from the moment you receive this document, a meeting between Boris Yeltsin, Ivan Silayev, Ruslan Khasbulatov, and Soviet President Mikhail Gorbachev. To involve Gennady Yanayev in the meeting.

2. To organize, within the next three days, a medical examination of the health of Soviet President Mikhail Gorbachev, involving experts from the World Health Organization. The government of the Russian Federation will assume the related hard-currency expenses.

3. To publish the results of the medical examination. If the president's health is normal, to urgently create conditions allowing him to resume his duties as Soviet president.

4. To lift without delay all restrictions on the work of the mass media of the Russian Federation, all the more so since no such limitations were introduced in other republics.

5. To lift the state of emergency on the entire territory of the Russian Federation for the period of the work of the Supreme Soviet of the Russian Federation; to ensure free departure from and arrival in Moscow of people's deputies of the Russian Federation.

6. To remove the troops to the places of their permanent dislocation.

7. To ensure that the president of the Russian Federation freely performs his duties in his Kremlin residence.

8. To urgently restore all types of communication for the normal functioning of the leaders of the Russian Federation.

9. To cut short all threats against the leaders of the Russian Federation and to ensure their immunity and freedom of movement.

10. To disband the illegal State of Emergency Committee and abolish all of its resolutions and instructions.

President of the Russian Federation Boris Yeltsin

Vice-President of the Russian Federation
Alexander Rutskoy

Chairman of the Council of Ministers
of the Russian Federation Ivan Silayev

Acting Chairman of the Supreme Soviet
of the Russian Federation Ruslan Khasbulatov

August 20, 1991

Resolution of the Presidium of the Supreme Soviet of the Russian Federation on the Convocation of an Extraordinary Session of the Supreme Soviet of the Russian Federation

On the night of August 18, the political situation in our country radically changed as a result of an anti-constitutional coup.

In accordance with the Constitution of the USSR, the state of emergency can be introduced only by the Supreme Soviet of the USSR or by the President of the USSR, by agreement with the republics, and in the absence of such agreement, by decision of the Supreme Soviet of the USSR, taken by at least two-thirds of its members. In view of the fact that the state of emergency was introduced in violation of the Constitution of the USSR, the actions of the so-called State of Emergency Committee represent a state coup.

The normal functioning of the constitutional bodies of power of the Russian Federation have been called into question.

In view of the current situation, the presidium of the Supreme Soviet of the Russian Federation hereby resolves:

1. To convene an extraordinary session of the Supreme Soviet of the Russian Federation on August 21, at 11:00, in the House of Soviets of the Russian Federation to discuss the political situation in the Russian Federation which has taken shape as a result of the coup.

2. To qualify the implementation of the resolutions of the so-called State of Emergency Committee as involvement in a state crime with all the ensuing consequences.

First Deputy Chairman of the
Supreme Soviet of the Russian Federation

Ruslan Khasbulatov
Moscow, House of Soviets of the Russian Federation
August 19, 1991
No. 1624-1

To the chairmen of the supreme soviets of the republics constituting the Russian Federation,

to the Chairmen of the territorial and regional soviets of people's deputies,

to the chairmen of the Moscow and Leningrad city soviets of people's deputies.

We are sending you the decrees of the President of the Russian Federation of August 19, 1991 and the appeal "To the Citizens of Russia" and "To the Servicemen of the Soviet Army," adopted in connection with the anti-constitutional state coup.

We are urging you to fully inform the population and unconditionally fulfill the provisions listed in the above-mentioned documents by all executives of establishments, organizations and enterprises.

Legal actions will be taken against leaders who do not take measures to implement the decrees of the President of the Russian Federation. The executives, implementing the resolutions of the anti-constitutional State of Emergency Committee, come under the Criminal Code of the Russian Federation and will be prosecuted.

Acting Chairman of the Supreme
Soviet of the Russian Federation Ruslan Khasbulatov

Moscow, House of Soviets of the Russian Federation
August 19, 1991
No. 15--58

Vice-President of the Russian Federation

To the Servicemen of the Armed Forces

Comrades, friends,

A military coup to establish a Stalinist-type dictatorship is being attempted. The state leaders responsible for the current situation in the country, aware of their forthcoming defeat and inevitable responsibility, have organized an anti-constitutional coup. The State of Emergency Committee which they have set up is plunging the country into the horrors of bloody war.

Comrades,

I am an officer of the Soviet army, a colonel, a Hero of the Soviet Union, who has fought in Afghanistan, and who knows the horrors of war, and I'm urging you, my colleagues, officers, soldiers and sailors, not to fight against the people, against your fathers, mothers, brothers and sisters. I appeal to your honor, reason and emotions. Today, the future of the country and its free and democratic development is in your hands.

Do everything to prevent bloodshed.

Give no support to the plotters. Make every effort to foil their criminal plans.

I am urging you to take the side of the legally-elected and democratic bodies of power: the President of the Russian Federation and the Council of Ministers of the Russian Federation.

Vice-President of the Russian Federation,
Hero of the Soviet Union Alexander Rutskoy

All-Union Council of Parents of Servicemen

August 19, 1991

TO ALL CITIZENS OF THE COUNTRY, TO THE WORLD COMMUNITY

The Presidium of the All-Union Council of Parents of Servicemen gives its full support to the appeal by the government of the Russian Federation.

We express our indignation at the conduct of a handful of adventurists who, of their own free will, have seized power and are trying to establish tyranny, violence and lawlessness. We declare the so-called committee which has come to power, and all of its resolutions and instructions to be illegal.

We urge the nation and the local bodies of power to give adequate rebuff to the putschists and to bring the country to its normal state.

We demand that President Gorbachev address the nation on national TV and radio, and that an extraordinary congress of people's deputies of the USSR be immediately convened.

We, soldiers' mothers, members of the All-Union Council of Parents of Servicemen, are urging you, officers, soldiers and sailors, and the entire personnel of the Soviet armed forces, to perform your civic duty and show self-control in this complicated situation. Do not take part in the reactionary coup!

We urge all people to go on a general indefinite strike until our demands are met.

We are convinced that the world community will objectively assess the cynical attempt by reactionary forces to accomplish a state coup.

All-Union Council of Parents
of Servicemen

Dear Muscovites,

Russia is undergoing a tragic moment in her history.

A group of plotters calling themselves a state of emergency committee, has accomplished an anti-constitutional putsch and is trying to establish its power. They have announced that the President of the USSR has been removed from power and that a state of emergency has been imposed on almost all of its territory.

We are confronted with a grave state crime---the betrayal of the people and the Constitution. The goal of the putschists is to undermine the newly-born democracy and throw the country back to totalitarianism. The committee members---the chief culprits of the grave crisis in society---act as political adventurists. The power which they have forcibly seized will bring much misfortune to our long-suffering nation and will lead the country into complete catastrophe. No one has ever managed to solve economic and political problems by arms and violence.

The actions of the putschists are undermining the prestige of our country in the eyes of the world community, deprive us of its support and are leading the country to complete isolation.

By decree of the President of the Russian Federation the activity of the committee has been qualified as illegal, and its orders as not liable for implementation. All the executive bodies of the USSR, including the KGB, the Ministry of Internal Affairs and the Ministry of Defense, operating on the territory of the Russian Federation will report directly to the President of the Russian Federation, elected by the people.

In this critical situation, the troops may try to block the House of Soviets of the Russian Federation. There is a direct danger of the legitimately elected leadership of the Russian Federation being overthrown.

Muscovites,

I am urging you not to recognize the self-imposed committee and not to implement its resolutions. Use all constitutional methods to do so---demonstrations, meetings and strikes. The House of Soviets of the Russian Federation and the republic's legitimate authorities must be given public protection.

The power of the people can be protected only by the people themselves.

Support the authorities you have elected in Moscow.

Show self-control and avoid clashes with the units of the Soviet army, the KGB and the Ministry of Internal Affairs which have been entangled in this criminal action. Explain to the soldiers, sergeants and officers the anti-democratic and anti-constitutional nature of the orders which they are being made to fulfill.

President of the Russian Federation Boris Yeltsin

August 19, 1991

Decree
By the President of the Russian Soviet Federative Socialist Republic

A state coup has been attempted; the President of the USSR who is the Supreme Commander of the USSR Armed Forces, has been removed from power. The Vice-President of the USSR, the Prime Minister of the USSR, the Chairman of the KGB and the ministers of defense and internal affairs, have joined the anti-constitutional body having thus committed a state crime. As a result of these actions, the legally elected executive bodies of the USSR have been paralyzed.

Taking into account the current situation, I hereby resolve:

1. Pending the convocation of an extraordinary congress of people's deputies of the USSR, to subordinate all of the USSR executive bodies operating on the territory of the Russian Federation, including the KGB, the Ministry of Internal Affairs, and the Ministry of Defense, to the president of the Russian Federation, elected by the people.

2. To temporarily charge the Russian Federation's State Security Committee, Ministry of Internal Affairs and State Committee for Defense with the functions of the corresponding bodies of the USSR operating in the Russian Federation.

All of the territorial and other bodies of the Ministry of Internal Affairs, the KGB and the Ministry of Defense operating in the Russian Federation shall instantly fulfill the decrees and orders of the Russian Federation's president, Council of Ministers, KGB, Ministry of Internal Affairs and State Committee for Defense.

3. To instruct all the bodies, executives and citizens of the Russian Federation to take urgent measures to exclude the implementation of any resolutions and instructions of the anti-constitutional State of Emergency Committee.

The executives implementing the resolutions of the above-mentioned committee, shall be freed from their duties in accordance with the Constitution of the Russian Federation. The bodies of the Procurator's Office of the Russian Federation shall take urgent measures to start legal action against such people.

President of the Russian Federation Boris Yeltsin

Moscow, Kremlin
August 19, 1991
No. 61

To the soldiers and officers of the USSR's
Armed Forces, KGB and Ministry of Internal Affairs

Servicemen,

Compatriots,

A state coup has been attempted. The President of the USSR who is the Supreme Commander of the Armed Forces of the USSR has been removed from power. The USSR's Vice-President, Prime Minister, Chairman of the KGB and ministers of defense and internal affairs have joined the unconstitutional body thus committing high treason, the gravest of state crimes.

The country has found itself under the threat of terror. The "order" promised to us by the self-imposed saviors of the Motherland will bring us tragedy, the suppression of dissidence, concentration camps and night arrests. A "better life" will remain a propaganda ruse.

Soldiers and officers of Russia,

In this tragic moment for Russia and for the whole of the country I appeal to you. Do not let anyone catch you in the net of mendacious promises and demagogic rhetoric about military duty. Do not become a blind instrument implementing the evil will of the adventurists who have trampled underfoot the Constitution and laws of the USSR.

I appeal to you, soldiers! Think of your relatives, friends and your people. In the dramatic moment of choice do not forget that you have taken an oath to be faithful to your people---the people against whom your arms are being turned.

One can build a throne of bayonets, but one will not be able to sit on it for long. There can and will not be any return to the past. The plotters' days are numbered.

Soldiers, officers and generals! An hour ago I appointed your comrade-in-arms, Colonel General K. Kobets, Chairman of the Russian Federation's Committee for Defense. I have passed a decree obliging the territorial and other bodies of the Russian Federation's Ministry of Internal Affairs, KGB and Ministry of Defense to instantly fulfill the orders of the President, KGB, Ministry of Internal Affairs and State Committee for Defense of the Russian Federation.

The clouds of terror and dictatorship have gathered above Russia and our entire country. But they cannot turn into an eternal night. Law will triumph in our country and our long-suffering people will regain freedom, once and for all.

Soldiers,

I am sure that in this tragic hour you will make the right choice. The honor and glory of the Russian arms will not be strained by human blood.

Boris Yeltsin
President of the Russian Federation
5:10 p.m.

CHRONICLE: THE FINALE OF THE PUTSCH

On the evening of August 20, thousands of Muscovites gathered at the building of the Supreme Soviet of Russia.

Russian MP V. Urazhtsev, arrested by the KGB the day before, arrived at the Supreme Soviet building. Nikolai Travkin was at home under KGB supervision.

9:00 p.m. An Izmailovo priest arrives to give the eucharist and blessing to the Russian Parliament's defenders.

The Road Police report that tanks are advancing towards the center of the city. Volunteers on guard at the White House are enrolling in militia corps and linking up in chains.

11:00 p.m. Groups of MPs head for Tushino and Khodynka, where the Tamanskaya and Kantemirovskaya divisions are stationed, to meet their commanders and persuade them to avoid all hostilities.

All the people inside the Russian Supreme Soviet receive gas masks.

The staff and enrollment of some Moscow military academies announce their readiness to swear allegiance to Russia.

Major-General Pavel Chernyshev, chief of the White House's defenses, receives the information that an attack is planned for 2 o'clock at night.

11:30 p.m. A. Mikhailov, a committee chief of maritime and river workers' union, arrives at the defense headquarters with a report that motor ships and barges with fire-extinguishing equipment have pulled up at the embankment.

Members of the Russian Government are being armed.

Midnight. Religious procession around the "White House."

A. Krasnov, chairman of the Krasnopresnensky district executive committee, notifies the defense headquarters that a Soviet Army regiment commander is seeking contact with the White House to render assistance.

First shots. All rush to the windows but can't see anything.

Helicopter pilots refuse to carry assault groups to seize the Parliament.

Radio interception: the time of assault is postponed till 4 o'clock in the morning. All anticipate KGB divisions.

The Vitebsk airborne division is moving along Kutuzov Prospect towards the White House. Alexander Rutskoi asks the headquarters to barricade the bridge.

0:06 a.m. First bursts of submachine gun fire from the side of the U.S. embassy. About 20 armored cars and some 5--6 tanks are approaching the White House from different sides.

0:10 a.m. The White House retaliates with tracer bullet bursts above the tanks. The lights are turned off and the reporters are forbidden to use flashes.

0:21 a.m. A phone report says that a barge carrying servicemen and cylinders, presumably for gas attacks or smoke screens, is moving along the Moskva River. Radio Liberty has reported with reference to Russian MPs that Lukyanov said Gorbachev was not an accomplice in the coup.

0:32 a.m. First victim. An armored car runs over a young man on Kalinin Prospect.

0:45 a.m. A crowd blocks the way to armored cars near Vosstaniya Square. Turret-mounted machine guns open fire vertically upwards with tracer bullets, dispersing the crowd. A column of armored personnel carriers enters the tunnel under the Kalinin bridge. One has the impression that the troops plan no frontal attack; they just want to encircle the White House and show a sign of strength.

Road police posts report that 80 pieces of military hardware are on their way from Kubinka to Moscow.

1:00 a.m. An armored car column is blocked in the tunnel under Novy Arbat with barricades of Ikaruses, garbage and sprinkling machines.

Russia's Deputy Minister of Health Deikin dispatches a car with drugs to the White House.

Servicemen in the city snatch the walkie-talkies from policemen.

1:15 a.m. Marksmen have been noticed on the roofs of multi-story buildings close to the White House.

1:30 a.m. The Moscow Military District headquarters reports that the Kantemirovskaya and Tamanskaya divisions have, in an act of disloyalty, withdrawn from the city. Only special-purpose and KGB troops remain in the city.

1:42 a.m. In the vicinity of the Udarnik Cinema armored car No. 536 opens fire on the barricades. Two people are either wounded or killed. A Molotov cocktail is thrown form a window, the armored car catches fire and the crew runs away.

2:00 a.m. Armored cars try to make a break through the barricades blocking the tunnel under Novy Arbat but are showered with Molotov cocktails. Two armored cars are set on fire and one starts rotating around its axis. A White House defender is run over and another one is shot in the head by submachine gun burst.

2:10 a.m. Moscow News contacts Russia's Secretary of State Gennadi Burbulis, who says: "The putschists are growing ever more impudent. We are surrounded by tanks and armored cars, but we are holding on. There are about

200 Moscow Soviet and Russian Parliament deputies in the building. Yeltsin is O.K."

2:12 a.m. The information transmitted by a radio station passing itself off as Moscow Echo in the early hours of August 21 is fictitious. As Moscow Echo correspondent Alexei Venediktov told us, the radio station was closed at 10:45 p.m. The reports by this false radio station, which exaggerated the number of victims, were obviously provocative.

2:45 a.m. Moscow News calls Burbulis, wondering if it is true that the military hardware has been withdrawn. Says Burbulis, "It would seem so. I contacted Yazov and Yanayev who said they would not be responsible for anything. At this moment I see Shevardnadze coming in.

3:05 a.m. The movement of KGB Vitebsk airborne division units in the direction of Moscow is noticed at the 40th kilometer of Minsk highway.

3:45 a.m. Moscow News phones Gennadi Burbulis again. The information of the past hour: the troops subordinate to the Ministry of Defense are leaving the city. There is however a report that the Vitebsk division is approaching the city. Burbulis calls KGB chief Kryuchkov and notifies him about this. Kryuchkov says: "I'll find out." Moscow News also asks Burbulis what Shevardnadze has come to the White House for. Answer: "He heard shooting and drove to the White House. We thanked him and asked him to return home. Yeltsin is still in the White House."

3:50 a.m. The White House radio station reports that a resolute assault may be undertaken in ten minutes. The chains of defenders tightly join ranks.

4:00 a.m. Judging by intercepted conversations, the attackers are trying to work out the attitude of the population towards the troops. Active action is not taken.

Communication between patrol cars and Russia's Ministry of the Interior is interrupted. Talks between the military stop.

4:15 a.m. Road police do not confirm the entrance of Vitebsk division units into Moscow.

4:30 a.m. The Yanayev-led Emergency Committee is in session at the Oktyabrskaya Hotel. Controversial reports about the results of the session are coming in. According to Colonel Tsalko, deputy commander-in-chief of the Russian armed forces, Vitebsk division units have stopped on the outskirts of Moscow, close to the Mozhaisky motel.

5:00 a.m. On the order of General Kalinin, commander of the Moscow military district, all district troops not stationed in Moscow are being withdrawn from the capital. His representative has arrived at the Moscow Soviet building to supervise the withdrawal of the troops.

5:00 a.m. According to Moscow Soviet sources, the Bryansk militia school is moving toward Moscow to help Yeltsin, while Pugo orders the Moscow police to disarm the cadets. Moscow News contacts Boris Pugo's reception-room. A secretary on duty says that he is unaware of this fact and that no such information is available.

5:25 a.m. Conversation with Burbulis. Says Burbulis: "According to our information, no troop progress has been noticed."

Two KGB brigades---one moving towards the center along Lenin Prospect, and the other along Minsk highway, turn back after the conversation with Burbulis. In the opinion of the Secretary of State, "the turning point has arrived. Individual outbursts are quite likely to take place but the situation is a great deal more optimistic."

5:40 a.m. Echo Moscow is on the air again. The radio station urges Muscovites to come out to defend the White House: all should be vigilant!

A. Krasnov, chairman of the Krasnopresnensky district executive committee, reports that the district KGB department is off the alert again.

7:00 a.m. Parliament deputies and local residents manage to halt technology from Moldova on Mozhaisk highway.

8:00 a.m. The Russian Parliament's defense headquarters appeal to everybody who cherishes freedom and democracy to come to protect the legitimately-elected Supreme Soviet of the republic.

11:00 a.m. A Russian Supreme Soviet session opens at the pre-set time. Boris Yeltsin is speaking to the deputies.

2:55 p.m. Moscow commandant Nikolai Kalinin, Commander-in-Chief of the Moscow military district, says that in the morning of August 21 the Collegium of the Defense Ministry gathered for a session but Defense Minister Dmitri Yazov was absent. They decided to call off the curfew in Moscow, withdraw troops from the capital and return them to their permanent bases.

Insert (bottom): On August 20--21, *Obshchaya Gazeta* (Common Newspaper) was released at the Commersant newspaper editorial office, entrusted by other newspapers with coordinating all their activities. Commersant thanks all organizations and citizens who have rendered unselfish (and any other kind of) aid in the compilation of Obshchaya Gazeta.

Telephone (editorial office): 941-09-00

Free Order No. 2121

Where Are You Going

A session of Russia's Supreme Soviet opened at 11:00 a.m. with a minute of silence to honor the perished defenders of the Russian Parliament. Boris Yeltsin makes a speech.

They decide to send to Silayev, Rutskoi and 10 other MPs to Lukyanov so that all of them might contact Gorbachev. The atmosphere inside and outside the Russian Parliament was rather tense, and although the failure of the night assault inspired some optimism, it was patently obvious that if the Emergency Committee decided to storm the White House again, it would be a more desperate attempt. No information about the Emergency Committee's activities had been available since the morning.

The turning point occurred at about 2 p.m.: Yeltsin said that, according to his sources, the eight putschists were heading for Vnukovo airport. A sudden feeling of confidence that everything was over set in---the junta was defeated by the unswerving resolve of the White House defenders to stand up to combat infantry vehicles and tanks with reinforced bars and Molotov cocktails.

Yeltsin asked the session to permit him to appeal to Vnukovo personnel and order the Russian KGB and Interior Ministry to block the putschists in Vnukovo. The permit was given. He also called for a vote to confer on him the right to dismiss the heads of the offices and institutions which supported the coup.

Controversial rumors followed. It was finally discovered that Gorbachev's dacha in Foros, blocked by a Sevastopol KGB regiment, was protected from the sea by the Black sea fleet supporting the Soviet President; communication with Mikhail Gorbachev could be maintained through ship-borne radio stations but contact was still not at hand.

It was learnt that the attempts to detain the plane with the putschists on board failed; the plane was heading for Simferopol. At first, it was believed that all 8 putschists had flown off.

According to partly unverified data, available, when this issue was passed on to the printing house and received from Pilot Union Vice-President Alexei Yeliseev, the putschists flew off in two planes. The first one (IL-62 No. 86540) took off at 2:18 p.m., with a planned landing at the military Saki airport at 4 o'clock. It was not quite clear who was on board; it apparently was carrying Yazov, Lukyanov and Ivashko. The next plane with putschists on board (TU-134 No. 65505) took off at 2:40 p.m. and landed in Saki at 4:40 p.m., with no clear details about the passengers (it had been discovered that Yanayev was not on board).

The first plane landed normally. The second one was allegedly told to land with its wheels locked, leading to the smashing of the rubber and the burning of the wheels. According to all available information, Yeltsin contacted the Air Force Commander-in-Chief, who gave the order for the plane to be pulled off the runway with tractors.

Rutskoi, Silayev, Bakatin and 10 Russian MPs set off at 4:00 p.m. to meet Gorbachev with a planned landing at 6:30 p.m. in Simferopol. No data is released about the fate of the putschists and the meeting of the Russian Parliament representatives with Gorbachev.

A major rally was held at the Russian Supreme Soviet building at 8 o'clock in the evening on August 21. Leningrad's Smena correspondent Georgi Urushadze said there that he had just contacted Gorbachev by phone. In the words of Urushadze, Gorbachev qualified the event as a coup d'etat and said that his meeting with the leadership of the Union Government would take place only after he had seen Yeltsin. Gorbachev's telephone was switched on at about 6 o'clock in the evening of August 21. Mikhail Gorbachev described the 72 hours of his captivity in Foros as "the stay at Brest fortress" and reported that all 12 bodyguards had remained loyal to him.

According to information received from the White House at 8:30 p.m., the Russian leadership adopted the decision to arrest Yanayev (which may, however, be understood by the investigative bodies merely as a recommendation). That first decision is explained by the fact that Yanayev was not a deputy and had no parliamentary immunity. The issue of Yanayev's arrest had not yet been discussed with Gorbachev.

Barricades are not pulled down until a special decision is received from the Russian government. The people who defended the White House have no intention of going away on the night of August 21--22. The defense has been reinforced with people, ammunition and additional fortifications. But it seems more than likely that the last night of the putsch is over.

THREE HOURS IN THE BUNKER

By Andrei Zhdankin

The further we are from those dramatic nights, when the White House defenders were prepared to sacrifice their lives, the greater is the evidence of the dimension of this would-be tragedy. Rossiyskaya Gazeta's correspondents got into Bunker No. 100, where the Russian President spent the night with his bodyguards, when the special KGB forces planned to storm the building. We followed the same route to the bunker as Boris Yeltsin in the company of security officers and partly reproduced the events of that night. They gave us the shivers.

We left the reception hall of the Russian President on the House of Soviets fifth floor, passed along a long corridor, descended a staircase and reached the basement. Yeltsin also had to walk, because in such situations lifts should be avoided at all costs. Other Russian leaders, bodyguards and several deputies accompanied him. The storm was to begin in 15 minutes.

The House of Soviets basement appeared to be colossal in size. We left behind the marble staircase. A huge safe, which lay on its side blocking the path against attackers, represented the last line of defense. Here the guards persuaded Boris Yeltsin to put on a bullet-proof vest. Personal weapons include a PSM pistol, accompanied by a gas mask with a short "proboscis." The guards don't wear these protective vests, as they are too costly, and are armed with submachine guns and Stechkin and PSM pistols. At last we came up to the huge armored door, which had a red wheel. That was Item No. 100. Many call it a bunker, but it was actually an ordinary bomb shelter.

About 40 people got inside. The wheel on the outer side of the door was removed. Our guide told us that hand grenades were useless against that door, while a specialist would know what to do. It was the last line of defense. As is to be expected, not everything was O.K. We had to break open a door, for we could not find the keys to it. There was no water in the bunker and the toilets were shut.

Two-tier plank beds are located on both sides of the long dark cement-laid corridor. The service room houses a self-contained power plant and the control panel of the life-support systems---ventilation, water-supply and lighting. Guards sat in front of the door, with ten on each bench. The door could be opened only from the inside and anybody who entered faced guns trained on them.

Those inside the bunker are well aware that they are, despite the weapons, thick walls and their courage, hostages. One can enter the bunker from the metro and the Russian Supreme Soviet reception room. A drain tunnel is located below this level. Even the guards do not know where it leads and what "visitors" may appear from it. The presidential security man who was our guide told us that the security service has a very thorough knowledge of the layout of all the service lines and drainage tunnels. (From the recent talk with the directors of Alfa group, we discovered that they had known for sure where Boris Yeltsin was and that the bunker only provided nominal protection.) The defenders feared most of all that gas might be released into the service lines. Yeltsin and the rest had no protection against gas other than the fairly inferior Soviet gas masks.

The large hall containing the Russian leaders had cement walls, a large table with telephones and chairs around it. We entered the presidential room, measuring in all a mere 10 square meters. It contained a writing-desk, armchair and sofa which was too small for our tall president, four chairs and a crate filled with gas masks. The desk telephones included: one channel for intercity calls, one for intercom and two channels for special communication. The room was made out of cement blocks and lined with monolithic concrete.

After spending less than three hours in the bunker, the President left and returned to his study: the guards could no longer keep him inside.

We walked the long corridors before we saw light. An uneasy thought overcame us: the President had only slight security guarantees. The bodyguards have no control over all the rooms in the huge building and cannot enter, even if the need arises, any of its rooms. The security service status has so far not been legalized. God will probably save use from another putsch, but still one never knows.

Today every room in the bunker is kept in working order and is ready for use at a moment's notice. True, the door which we had broken down was repaired only a week later. Our conversation with the presidential security service men revealed that there are still far too many weak spots in the security system. Personal courage will resolve all the problems.

THE WHITE HOUSE IS WAITING FOR THE REDS

By Ilya Vais, Mikhail Kamensky, Leonid Miloslavsky

The storming of the White House began shortly after midnight. Having broken through the first line of defenses, the tanks stopped. According to preliminary estimates by correspondents who worked in and around the White House, there were five casualties: people tried to stop the tanks and armored personnel carriers.

On the first morning of the putsch, the House of Soviets of the Russian Federation on Krasnopresnenskaya Embankment (the White House) looked strangely peaceful: there were neither tanks nor official black Volga cars there. But by noon it became clear that neither side had forgotten about the White House: tanks settled at the facade and a meeting began immediately afterwards. Standing on a tank, Russian President Boris Yeltsin gave his first public assessment of the coup.

There were not many people at the meeting, around three thousand, because the White House had not yet become the focus of public attention. Democrats had concentrated in Manezhnaya Square and in Tverskaya Street. As the rumors of the possible arrest of Yeltsin and the impending storm of the White House spread, defenses grew stronger and became more organized. By the evening there were about 10,000 people who had built barricades.

Next day the creation of the volunteer corps was initiated.

By the morning of August 20, the defenders had completed the erection of barricades. Next to anti-personnel barricades concrete anti-tank barriers appeared, and the roads leading to the White House were blocked by trucks loaded with sand. The conscription of volunteers (with the exception of women and children) began in the afternoon. They were divided into hundreds and headed by mostly demobilized servicemen. Volunteer doctors and nurses served in a small mobile hospital. The collection of food and money to buy it was very lively: the people donated willingly and as much as they could. Nobody bothered to write down the names of donors. Fresh water was stored up in buckets, canisters and jars. Disposable glasses were located nearby. Women were not allowed through the barricades.

At three o'clock in the afternoon a column of 150--200 people arrived from Zelenograd, most of them equipped with gas masks. A cargo taxi brought several Xerox machines to make leaflets and duplicate statements of the Russian government. Steel rods and pipes cut into convenient clubs were scattered around the building and along the barricades. The stones from the paved memorial Krasnopresnensky Bridge, which served so well during the 1905 revolution, were again taken out. The defenders of the White House who stood close to the building checked the contents of big bags and coffers.

In the evening many young, strong men appeared in the crowd. They proclaimed that they had never been party members and called on the people to disperse. "Gorbachev and Yeltsin have not done a good thing for the people," they argued," while the new regime has not done anything bad to you."

At five in the afternoon the White House radio announced that they had intercepted a radio order of the military command on the storming of the White House. At 5:15 p.m. this information was reaffirmed by Ruslan Khasbulatov---Anatoly Lukyanov told him over the telephone that there was an order to clear the square by "raising the blockade." Men in the White House were issued arms, women left the building. Then the men were told to leave the building, get into a bus and move towards the troops, which were said to be moving along Leningradskoye Highway and Bolshaya Gruzinskaya Street. Their task was to convince the soldiers not to shoot. Those who remained in the White House waited for the appearance of assault groups from the underground (Metro) and air (paratroopers).

More than 50,000 defenders standing before the White House listened to radio relays about the coming assault, and waited for it. The tanks did not appear.

At 7:30 p.m. several teachers of the Moscow Radio-Technical School brought 240 gas masks, the entire stock of the school, which was kept there for civil defense lessons. At the same time, 30 doctors started distributing gauze, to be used in case of tear gas or toxic attacks. Fifty ambulances surrounded the volunteers. These preparations for the storm went on to the accompaniment of prayers by a group of Krishnaites and radio addresses in support of the defenders of the White House. Mstislav Rostropovich announced that he had come to the White House from the Congress of Compatriots and would not leave the building whatever happened.

At 10 p.m. the defenders were still waiting for the assault to begin. Nobody left their posts. Only a part of the Russian government, led by Silayev, left for the "secret headquarters," as was announced, in order to continue their work there.

The assault began after midnight.

At 1 a.m. about 15 armored personnel carriers and 30 tanks started moving towards the White House from Kalininsky Prospekt. They easily went over the barricades in Kalininsky Prospekt, and it is rumored that one person died in the process. A column of tanks was advancing from Sadovoye Ring. Shooting was heard at the White House. The White House Radio called on civilians not to fight back in order to avoid casualties. They should only protect themselves, while those deployed in the building proper were to shoot without warning at anybody who tried to storm it. The shooting was mostly done from handguns.

A column of infantry fighting vehicles, deployed in the tunnel at the U. S. Embassy, attempted to speed through to the embankment. Their way was blocked with several rows of trolleybuses, but the first vehicle broke through. The defenders moved the trolleybus back into its former position, but the fighting vehicle again broke through, after several pushes. The defenders poured gasoline on the vehicle and set it on fire. The crew of the vehicle and the defenders tried to put out the fire, which spread to nearby trolleybuses. Water was splashed on the fire from a bucket, a cistern and bottles from the window of a nearby first-floor flat. The fire was put out in about twenty minutes, and those who helped extinguish it retreated back to their side of the barricades.

Another column of armored vehicles which had moved towards the White house stopped a hundred meters away from it. A group of Russia's deputies approached the soldiers and tried to convince them not to storm the building. The deputies said that they had failed in their mission, not because of irreconcilable differences but because the soldiers were drunk.

According to preliminary estimates of correspondents who were in the White House and around it, five people died trying to stop the armored vehicles and tanks.

Horror, Yazov is About!

The map of the deployment of government troops in Moscow, drafted in the emergency situation headquarters of the Moscow City Soviet, for 4 p.m. of August 20

1. Krasnokholmsky Bridge: three T-80 tanks
2. On the other side: two T-80 tanks
3. Gorky Park: four T-80 tanks
4. Chkalov St., Vysokoyauzsky Bridge: two T-80s each
5. Radio St. at the embankment: two T-80 tanks
6. Bolshaya Krasnokazarmennaya Square: four T-80s and two infantry fighting vehicles (IFV)
7. Bolshoi Kamenny Bridge: three T-80s on either end
8. Zvenigorodskoye Highway: eight armored personnel carriers (APC)
9. Kachalov St., Kudrinskaya St.: seven T-80s and three APCs

10. Nikitskiye Gate: nine APCs
11. Zubovskaya Square: six T-60s, two IFV-2s and one IFV-1
12. Krymskaya Square: four T-80s and one APC
13. Smidt Bridge: eight T-80s
14. Pushkin Square: ten APCs
15. 25 October St. and Revolution Square: 25 APCs and one armored reconnaissance assault vehicle
16. Chekhov St., Pushkin Square: ten APCs
17. Taganskaya Square: four T-80s

Moscow Center: Nobody Feared Men With Riffles in Daylight

August 19

9 a.m.: Emergency situation headquarters established in the Moscow City Soviet (tel.: 229-2083)

Noon: Several thousand people gathered in Manezhnaya Square. Deputies of the Moscow City Soviet called on people to support Yeltsin via a general strike.

12:30 p.m.: The demonstrators blocked the way to eight APCs of the Taman Division, who had approached by way of the Okhotny Ryad, with trolleybuses. The meeting passed off in an unfriendly but more or less calm atmosphere.

1:24 p.m.: The army occupied and closed the Central Telegraph. The 27th Sevastopol Brigade of the KGB spetsnaz forces occupied Manezhnaya St. on the side of the Bolshoi Kamenny Bridge---but let through tourist groups visiting the Armory.

2–4 p.m.: About 20 APCs and 15 army trucks settled in Manezhnaya Square. Twelve T-80s tanks of the Taman Division were entrenched at the Bolshoi Kamenny and Zamoskvoretsky bridges. OMON (five buses brought 25 men each) and motor-rifle troops (seven buses with 35 men each) surrounded Red Square. In the square proper stood 15 trucks with militiamen.

5 p.m.: Soldiers started pushing back the crowd from the square; the operation lasted seven hours and passed off in an atmosphere of mutual understanding. However, APCs added a jarring note by speeding onto the square from Herzen Street. The people tried to stop them, and consequently two APCs crashed into each other. Nobody was hurt.

August 20

Noon: At the meeting at the Moscow City Soviet, Alexander Yakovlev, Gavriil Popov, Eduard Shevardnadze and Sergei Stankevich said that the members of the self-imposed Committee for the State of Emergency were criminals. Yakovlev said that "the counter-revolution which the Bolsheviks had contemplated for so long, has happened."

2 p.m.: Demonstrators moved from the Moscow City Soviet to the Russian Parliament by Sadovoye Ring. The troops did not stop them.

On August 20 Viktor Kuzin, of the Commission on Law of the Moscow City Soviet, called Leonid Zolotov, chief of staff of the Moscow Military District, and interviewed him on behalf of *Commersant*. Zolotov said that troops have been deployed in Moscow in order to fight all those who built barricades. We know who these people are, Zolotov said, "idle hands with nothing better to do." He did not say a word about the strength of the troops deployed in Moscow but mentioned that their number had halved since the previous day. Zolotov agreed with Kuzin that there was not need to move in so many troops and frighten the people. He added that he reported his opinion to the leaders of the Defense Ministry, but to no avail. The chief of staff said that the troops would be withdrawn from Moscow only after the barricades had been pulled down and the defenders of the White House had dispersed.

TANKS ON KRASNAYA PRESNYA: WHOSE FLAGS?

By Igor Svinarenko

In the evening of August 19 the first happy news spread among the defenders of the White House: ten of "our" tanks, that is, those crews who sided with Yeltsin, were heading towards it. The tanks were welcomed with flowers. Around 11 in the evening five T-76 tanks passed through the barricades, which were dismantled for the purpose, to the applause of the people.

The celebration of the "deserters" arrival was long and warm. Cigarettes, water melons, sausage, canned meat and other foods were handed over to the tanks while the people around shouted "hurray." Tricolor Russian flags were hoisted on the antennas and flowers hung from the tanks' guns. Girls climbed onto the turrets and kissed the soldiers, clearly with patriotic feeling. Up to 15 people climbed onto some tanks. On August 20, when the tankmen fastened the hatches in order to sleep after the night's fuss, volunteers protected their sleep by preventing people from climbing onto the tanks.

In short, the military were welcomed like heroes, gallant defenders of the Russian Parliament who sided with the legitimate government. Nikolai Maslov, Rutskoy's aide, told *Commersant* that the heroes were from the tank battalion of the 1st Guards Sevastopol Regiment of the Taman Division (commander Leontyev, chief of staff Yevdokimov).

But in the late hours of August 19 and small hours of August 20 the tankmen were not sure that they would actually defend the White House. They told a correspondent that they came there because they were ordered to do so by their commander. The order did not make any mention about the defense of the Parliament. When asked if they would defend the building if troops loyal to Yanayev attempt to seize it, the officers answered evasively that they did not have any ammunition. However, they did not rule out that shells and bullets could be delivered very soon.

Lieutenant Alexander (the military preferred not to give their names) from tank #111 said that he is "a Russian officer and took the oath of allegiance to the people and the legal power. As far as I understand, the legal power now is represented by Yeltsin, and God only knows what will happen next." Soldiers mostly kept silent and could not even formulate the order they had been given.

Around midnight 27 armored assault vehicles advanced on the Russian Parliament. This alerted the defenders of the White House who were prepared to regard the newcomers as an assault force. But after 1 a.m. Gennady Burbulis, Secretary of State of the Russian Federation, assured them that the newcomers are on "our" side. It was a unit of the Tula Regiment (commander Colonel Kobelev) of the Ryazan Airborne Division, who sided with the legitimate power. Burbulis said that "the President of Russia trusts the battalion servicemen, I trust them, and you should trust them, too." He asked the people to "support all movements and maneuvers which they (the troops) would undertake" because "these movements are controlled by General Kobets on the instructions of President Yeltsin."

The people let the 27 vehicles through the barricades with the same warm welcome they had afforded to the tanks. They were offered food and water, the people shouted "Thanks" and "For Yeltsin~" The paratroopers were rather restrained and mostly evaded the question, which was asked more than once: "Will you shoot at the people if you are ordered to?" However, some of them retorted, with irritation: "And what if we are not ordered to shoot?" The people did not quarrel with the paratroopers but tried to delicately win them over to their side.

When asked directly by a correspondent if his unit had sided with the Russian government, Senior Lieutenant Sergei of the Airborne Forces, replied: "Honestly, I don't know anything about this. I am just fulfilling an order." Then amateur propagandists told the Lieutenant about the tragic fate of the servicemen who had been tried in Nuremberg for fulfilling bad orders.

Soon a messenger ran up to the paratroopers and relayed the order of Rutskoy, not Kobets, to take position around the building. The paratroopers complied. However, as it turned out the next day, when moving around the square and leaving it in the morning of August 20, they followed the orders not of Rutskoy but of their own commanders. The defenders of the White House for the first time wondered whose orders the paratroopers would fulfill in a critical situation? Their commanders must have thought the same thing---according to one version, they called the paratroopers off because they did not trust them. Anyway, the headquarters of Kobets could not give another explanation. According to information which *Commersant* correspondents acquired from military sources, which could be trusted, not a single serviceman stated officially that he had sided with the Russian government. The tanks and paratroopers came to the White House in compliance with the deployment plan.

Late in the evening of August 19 and in the small hours of August 20 Russian deputies toured military units deployed in Moscow Region trying to win them over to their side. But the rumors that the Taman Division and the Air Force sided with Yeltsin as a result of propaganda efforts and the growth of consciousness, were not confirmed. According to some information, the most the deputies managed to do was convince the units they visited not to interfere.

HOW THE THREE YOUNG MEN WERE KILLED

It happened between 00:04 a.m. and 00:43 a.m. on August 21 in downtown Moscow, almost in front of the U.S. embassy, at the entrance to the tunnel under New Arbat Avenue.

One version: two infantry combat vehicles managed to breach a barricade of trolley-buses at the tunnel entrance in Smolensk Square. The people around dashed forward to fill the gap. As more vehicles appeared to crush the barricade, Dmitri Komar jumped on vehichle number 536. Some witnesses say he was shot point-blank from an open hatch, others argue that the lid of the back hatch flung open as the vehicle bumped against the barricade hitting him on the head and press him dead against the armor.

Several people rushed to pull Dmitri off the car. Among them was Vladimir Usov who was run over by the vehicle backing up.

A Molotov cocktail hurled at the vehicle set it on fire and the crew jumped out. The officer who tried to clear the way for his soldiers through the raging crowd began to fire in the air. Bursts of upward submachine gun fire came from another infantry combat vehicle nearby. It was then that Ilya Krichevsky was killed, but it is not certain what direction the bullet came from.

The investigation may last for days or weeks. We have no right to charge the soldiers who were inside that vehicle. But we ought to imagine their state of mind and feelings. The soldiers are obliged to perform orders. Moreover those fellows were armed officers who, under the oath of enlistment, had to obey unconditionally. To say nothing of the fact that those 18--20 year-old youngsters were amidst an angry storm of people.

The three young men who were killed were former soldiers. Two of them were the sons of military men---a Major and a Rear-Admiral. That was the will of destiny. So judge for yourself whose side the Army is on.

The interrogation is being held by six investigators: four of them are associates of the Moscow criminal investigation department and two are from the Moscow military garrison. Only the military can assess whether the vehicle was in order and, consequently, the reason for the death of Vladimir Usov. It is essential to know whether the vehicle that reversed needed repairs or was in perfect working order. And who shot at Ilya Krichevsky? A lot of weapons should undergo ballistic examination. It is very important to find out if the action complied with the orders and the mission set.

All the servicemen who were inside the eighteen infantry combat vehicles are identified. The crew of vehicle No. 536---all four soldiers and the Sergeant aged 18--20---have been interrogated. In the early hours of August 19, the driver mechanics were alerted and the rest were driven to the city later in the day. The crews were formed here, in Moscow.

The soldiers had no information. They were in Moscow for the first time though had served for a year in its suburbs. They spent all of Monday idle in their vehicles in Medvedkovo and felt that something was wrong. But what? There was nobody around, no people approached them to explain anything. On Tuesday, they received the order to patrol Sadovoye Ring. What happened after that is detailed in yesterday's issue of your newspaper. I should add something.

When the antenna of infantry combat vehicle No. 536 broke, it tried to round vehicle No. 535 squeezed by the crowd; the crew had no communication with the outer world. Look, here are triplex observation devices. What can you see through this network of cracks in full darkness? The soldiers could not make out what happened to the hatch and what all the bumps on the roof meant.

The situation was terrible and difficult to evaluate in their isolation. As the soldiers got out of the blazing vehicle they were showered with stones and bottles.

Given the lack of communication and visibility, there could have been many more victims. Let us be objective. Shouts of "Pound the soldiers!" and "Blow up everything!" were numerous. Happily, there were sober people who tried to reason and prevent any acts of lynching.

Yes, when struggling their way through the crowd, all five men shot pistols and submachine guns. They had not been warned that firing upwards in the air on a street crowded with buildings spelt danger. Incidentally, one of the bullets burst into a window on the fifteenth floor of a block of flats.

Full ignorance was aggravated by total unpreparedness for action in such a situation. The guys lacked any experience of driving in a big city even in peacetime.

The guilt of these fellows is not yet proved but I want to say that the blame should by all means be laid with those who issued military orders and authorized the entry of military hardware into Moscow. We shall have to interrogate the command of the Moscow military district and perhaps even the more high-ranking military.

I was shaken by one observation. The Sergeant saw the issue of Moskovsky Komsomolets on my table with the article about the guys killed. He was shocked as he learned for the first time who were those fellows caught under the tracks of their vehicle. I saw the eyes and hands of the soldiers: they were shaken by what had happened.

Dmitri Komar

23 years of age. Born to the family of a regular officer. After finishing school in 1986 was called up for military service. Spent six months at a training center in Lithuania, then was sent to Afghanistan. Returned home in February 1989; received five medals; shell-shocked.

Worked as an auto-loader driver at the Interyer specialized industrial-trading association (SPTO).

Lived in the Istra District. Moscow Region.

On the night of August 20--21, 1991, when defending the government building of the Russian Federation, he received a craniocerebral injury and was smashed by the tracks of an airborne combat vehicle.

Hero of the Soviet Union (posthumously).

Ilya Krichevsky

Born in 1963 in Moscow to a family of architects.

Architect, artist, poet and theater amateur.

After graduating from college served in the army (tank forces). Back at home, started to work at a design institute.

On the night of August 20--21, he was killed when defending the government building of the Russian Federation (cerebral injury and bullet wounds to the chest).

Hero of the Soviet Union (posthumously).

Vladimir Usov

Born 1954.

Father---Alexei Arsentyevich, retired rear-admiral.

After finishing school served in the Navy on the Baltic.

Worked as an economist at the Icom joint enterprise.

Married, daughter Marina, 14.

On the night of August 20--21, he was smashed by the tracks of an airborne combat vehicle.

Hero of the Soviet Union (posthumously).

3SD13M911003SI62

EXCERPTS FROM SPEECHES MADE AT THE FUNERAL MEETING

Mikhail Gorbachev:

It is hard to speak, as I look at their young faces and their parents standing nearby. Allow me to bow low, not only on my own behalf, but on yours, the whole country's and on behalf of all Russians in particular before the three young men who sacrificed their lives and stood up against those who wanted to return the country to the gloomy days of totalitarianism, to throw it into an abyss and lead it to a bloody massacre. I am eternally grateful to their parents. This is all we can say in condolence at this trying hour. To commemorate the actions of these young men, all of us consider ourselves bound to continue following the chosen road, and continue as soon as possible along the road of normal development and the improvement of our lives, no matter how hard this may be. There will be no pardon for the putschists. Today I signed a decree conferring the title of Hero of the Soviet Union posthumously upon Dmitry Komar, Ilya Krichevsky and Vladimir Usov. We are bidding our last farewell to genuine citizens. They have done their utmost.

Elena BONNER:

These three days were not days or hours, but a whole epoch whereby we covered an immeasurably longer path. As an elderly person, I can do no more than offer words of consolation to the parents of these boys. We must ensure that their sons did not give up their lives for nothing. All of us together must as a whole country prevent the elected government from distorting the facts and confusing us. The army must train soldiers, rather than murders. When I say this I do not mean to put the army against the people. If I say that the CPSU must be made answerable for the current situation in the country and the morality of the people, this does not mean that I demand that millions of honest working people be held responsible. We must learn to think for ourselves and learn how to become citizens. One hundred and thirty-two years ago Abraham Lincoln opened a cemetery for the victims of the American Civil War. They were buried together---both those who died for the cause of freedom and those who died in defense of slavery. We must not forget that the boys now serving in the army, the spetsnaz and OMON troops, are all our boys, too. We will have to learn a lot---genuine humaneness, loyalty to the concepts of freedom and democracy. I want to tell people of my generation, those who lived through the Second World War, not to long for order, that is the concept of order that the SS-men called Ordnung. We should desire the order which symbolizes freedom and democracy.

Egidijus BISKAUSKAS:

These three boys were protecting not only Russia's parliament, but also the parliament of Lithuania. We know that there cannot be a free Lithuania without a free Russia. You gave up your lives for our freedom and yours.

Robert STRAUSS, U.S. Ambassador to the USSR:

I am speaking on President Bush's behalf. More than two hundred years ago a great patriot of ours said when addressing God: "Give me Liberty or give me death." And ever since then many Americans who came to face that choice have made that great sacrifice. Just like these young people did. The justice of their cause does not minimize the common grief. All week the American people were in a state of shock with you, watching with admiration the defense of the "White House" and all that it symbolizes. We share your grief and mourn over the price paid for the just cause.

IMMEDIATE POST-PUTSCH EVENTS

YELTSIN SHOULD MEET WITH GORBACHEV NO LATER THAN AUGUST 21

The plenipotentiary delegation of the President of the Russian Federation, consisting of Vice President Alexander Rutskoy, Prime Minister Ivan Silayev and acting Chairman of the Supreme Soviet of the Russian Federation Ruslan Khazbulatov, conducted talks in the Kremlin with Chairman of the USSR Supreme Soviet Anatoly Lukyanov. The legitimate representatives of authority demanded that: a medical examination of Gorbachev be conducted within three days, a meeting of Russia's leadership with him should be organized after the lapse of 24 hours, all threat against Russia's leadership should cease immediately, troops should be moved to places of their deployment, the state of emergency should be lifted and the disbandment of the State Committee for the State of Emergency (GKChP) should be declared.

At that time, the legal status of Russia's "truce envoys" was backed up by the support from a regiment of the Ryazan airborne troops, a battalion of the Sevastopol mechanized infantry regiment and a battalion of the Taman division. The commanders of an other two units came to Yeltsin.

Alexander Rutskoy briefly commented on the visit to the putschists in a public speech: "We have presented our legitimate demands to Lukyanov. In our presence, he brought them to the notice of the so-called committee."

Rutskoy emphasized that the GKChP was given 24 hours to meet the demands. Russia's Vice President spoke specially about Lukyanov whose position "can be understood, because he himself returned to Moscow on August 19." During the talks, Anatoly Ivanovich, as a lawyer, admitted that many provisions of the GKChP documents did not correspond with Soviet law; he stated his intention to look into the matter at the Presidium of the USSR Supreme Soviet. According to Rutskoy, Lukyanov intended to insist on Gorbachev's presence at this meeting. Anatoly Ivanovich was luckier than others and had a telephone conversation with the President of the USSR. According to the information he had, Gorbachev "is alive, healthy, but has slight ailments: high blood pressure and radiculitis."

HOW THE TV-TRANSMITTER APPEARED ON THE WHITE HOUSE ROOF

By V. Mirolevich, *Izvestia*'s special correspondent

As is known, from the very first day of the putsch the "White House" had its own "voice," an amateur radio station. Aware of the complexity and danger of broadcasting under the threat of the putschists' reprisals, we knew all the same that it was feasible. On August 21 Russian television livened up. Russian Vesti (News Flash) broadcasts started up from the White House's own television studio. Where did the TV-transmitter brought into an embattled fortress come from?

From Voronezh. The manufacturers are now back home from Moscow and executing a new order for the Russian television and radio broadcasting company, producing another 1,000 unique sets.

On August 19 the Voronezh-based firm Sintez (it was set up 12 months ago by specialists from the Zarya NPO and the Radio Electronics School) was asked by Moscow to ensure television and radio communication for the Russian Government. The specialists at once got the hint and "went underground." They closed all the doors and, without leaving the room, did the job in little over 24 hours.

In the evening of August 20, they loaded the transmitter into the car of deputy director Nikolai Khokhlov and speeded off to Moscow. Khokhlov was accompanied by specialists Andrei Kamshilin, Oleg Pargachevski and Sergei Bryakov. The transmitter was carried in an ordinary shopping bag: unlike studio transmitters, which occupy an entire room, they produce compact ones in Voronezh.

Those people knew what awaited them if it had been discovered an ordinary car was bringing to Moscow. But all went well and they reached the place where they were expected. They eventually arrived at the White House to install the transmitter.

They could see everything from the roof---the snipers in the windows of the house opposite, unarmed defenders in the street below, tanks and armored cars on the approaches to the barricades. Guarded by a special sniper and black berets, they built their own priceless "barricade." From their barricade they could show viewers what was really going on.

The foreign newsmen present on the scene were delighted when the transmitter began to work on the makeshift antenna---an iron ladder. (They did not know that in his time Khokhlov had defended a dissertation on antennas.) For more than 24 hours they stood on watch on the White House roof. Now there were five of them: Nikolai Sinyukov joined them later with a powerful transmitter made by the same firm.

What's more, since the Voronezh team with their equipment worked near the flagstaff, they were the ones, that is---Nikolai Khokhlov, Andrei Kamshilin, Oleg Paragchevski, Sergei Bryakov and Nikolai Sinhukov---who, after the 73-year interval, raised the first tricolor above the Russian White House.

(Voronezh)

THEY DID NOT FORGET TO SWITCH OFF THE TV AND RADIO

By Sergei Mitrofanov

At 4:30 a.m. on August 19, an accredited representative of one of the members of the State of Emergency Committee called another accredited representative from the administration of Russian TV and warned him about the impending coup. Neither of them gave their names to our correspondent for reasons of secrecy.

All TV staffers went to work as usual only to discover that there would be no broadcasting because all TV transmitters in the Ostankino office had been unplugged and all channels were showing Channel 1 programs. According to some reports, it was done at 8 a.m. "Some people came and tore out all the electric plugs."

All communication with Ostankino was cut off. The editors received the correspondent's request to contact Ostankino with a chuckle. He tried to do it himself but got no answer.

At 10 a.m. the republican TV stations went dead. The republican channels were guided to retranslators put on the perimeter of Moscow. The retranslators used to jam out stations and, in a sense, performed this role again. Although Western radio stations were not jammed in general, any live (by phone) broadcast from Moscow was.

A Russian radio broadcast was to begin at 2 p.m., but never did, as the transmitter was located in Ostankino. The editors continued to work as usual, analyzing the information as it came in and trying to transmit it to Western radio stations. A large black pistol was lying on the table of editor Alexander Nenashev. At 4 p.m. a fan of Russian Radio called and asked him to specify something they had broadcast last time. This caused a hysterical laughter.

"Echo Moscow" began to work at 7 a.m. and broadcasted official reports alternating them with music for nearly 40 minutes. At 7:40 a.m. plain-clothes men entered the editorial office and asked the editors to stop the broadcast. Sergei Korzun, editor-in-chief, said that his journalist's ethics prevented him from doing so. Then the plain-clothes men cut off the electricity and sealed the room. The transmitter of the "Echo Moscow" was also cut off from the editorial office since the announcers had a wire connection with the transmitter and the wire was removed from the electric circuit.

It was reported from Ostankino that the program listings for next week were being made and that they included neither Russian Radio nor Russian Television.

On the night of August 19--20, the situation in the mass media gradually began to change. Radio Russia fixed an antenna on the roof of the House of the Soviets and began to work. They made several broadcasts in Russian and English. The transmitter is located in the building itself. One of the radio beams is directed at America but nobody knows whether it receives the signal. Programs are broadcasted at the frequencies of 21 and 16 meters in the morning, 42 and 61 meters in the daytime and 22 and 42 meters at night. At 1 p.m. "Echo Moscow" resumed its work. According to its editors, the Ministry of Communications, where the transmitter is located, was defeated by purely bureaucratic means, namely the permission of Moscow Soviet. The building is guarded by Russian riot police.

At Russian TV the situation remains unchanged. They cannot broadcast their programs bypassing Ostankino. Now they negotiate the broadcasting of the session of the Supreme Soviet of the Russian Federation. The negotiations are held by Khasbulatov and Rutskoi on the one hand, and Lukyanov, on the other. The administration of the Central TV has adopted a guarded attitude. To quote a Central TV executive, in this situation one should either leave Central TV or execute the orders of the leaders in power. "We can't change our positions overnight," he said. "Now the Democrats call for Gorbachev to resign, and now they want him back."

WILL GORBACHEV LEAVE THE CPSU?

By Yevgeny Krasnikov

The majority of the country's political parties and movements have already expressed their opinion of Mikhail Gorbachev and the State of Emergency Committee which is an alternative to him. Only the CPSU, which is the ruling party, remains silent. Apparently, the party leaders do not want the events to be regarded as a communist plot.

Our correspondent was told by the circles close to the central party leadership that on August 19 the party mass media had been recommended to reserve their judgement of the situation. This recommendation was carried out. On August 19 and 20 the press centers of the CPSU Central Committee and the Central Committee of the Communist Party of the Russian Federation flatly refused to give any information about the actions of Communist leaders.

However, judging by unofficial reports, a fierce fight went on at the time between President Gorbachev's supporters and opponents in the party leadership. On August 19, a member of the CPSU Central Committee, who preferred to stay anonymous, told a Commersant correspondent that an extraordinary plenary meeting of the CPSU Central Committee was scheduled for August 20. Although the agenda was usual, "On the situation in the country and the party," the meeting was being convened to discuss the political position of Comrade Gorbachev, General Secretary of the CPSU Central Committee.

However, the plenary meeting never took place. A meeting of the Secretariat of the CPSU Central Committee was held in the evening of August 19. Obviously, the meeting resolved to postpone the plenary meeting of the Central Committee until the end of the session of the USSR Supreme Soviet. One of the democratic Communists, members of the CPSU Central Committee, explained this by the fact that Gorbachev's supporters had refused to attend the plenary meeting and that consequently there was no quorum. A meeting of the Politburo of the CPSU Central Committee was instead held on August 20. According to some reports, it was enlarged and held jointly with the Politburo of the Central Committee of the Communist

Party of the Russian Federation. The joint statement of the two Politburos which gives a guarded approval of the introduction of the state of emergency and the organization of the State Committee for the State of Emergency, is to be published on August 21.

"Owing to the illness of the General Secretary" his work may be assigned to his deputy Vladimir Ivashko, not as acting president but in compliance with the decision of the Politburo. It must be the only way to remove Gorbachev from the party leadership as well. Judging by the results of the two latest plenary meetings held in April and July, Gorbachev and his policies enjoy the support of the overwhelming majority of Central Committee members. In accordance with the Party Rules, only a congress has the right to accept the resignation of the General Secretary.

Apparently, Gorbachev's opponents in the party leadership will try to postpone the convocation of the plenary meeting of the CPSU Central Committee as long as possible and hold it only when the political situation will become clear. If Gorbachev's opponents win by that time, members of the Central Committee will hardly dare rebel and defend "their beloved General Secretary."

A Putsch at the Working People's Request?

The "DATA" Information Agency reports that on August 20, 1991 the All-Union Public Opinion Center, in cooperation with the Public Opinion Fund, is holding a survey in Russia. Information is coming from different cities. In Leningrad, Voronezh, Krasnoyarsk and Lvov, 1,438 people have been polled according to the quota principle.

1. Do you consider the actions of the State of Emergency Committee to be legitimate?

	Voronezh	Krasnoyarsk	Leningrad	Lvov
Yes	28	12	23	13
No	49	76	54	71
Don't know	23	12	23	16

2. Will the State of Emergency Committee improve or aggravate the economic situation in the country?

	Voronezh	Krasnoyarsk	Leningrad	Lvov
Improve	24	9	19	12
Aggravate	38	77	46	59
Don't know	38	14	35	29

3. Will mass repressions be initiated now?

	Voronezh	Krasnoyarsk	Leningrad	Lvov
Yes	57	61	71	62
No	26	23	19	21
Don't know	17	16	10	17

4. What's your attitude towards Yeltsin's appeal for an indefinite strike?

	Voronezh	Krasnoyarsk	Leningrad	Lvov
I support it	30	57	40	42
I don't support it	49	33	31	38
Don't know	21	10	29	20

MUAMMAR AL-GADDAFI AND SADDAM HUSSEIN ARE THE ONLY ONES TO HAVE RECOGNIZED THE STATE OF EMERGENCY COMMITTEE

By Oleg Myshkin

"The Soviet leadership hopes that the temporary emergency measures will meet with the understanding of the peoples, governments and the UN." (Excerpted from the Address to Heads of State and Government, and the UN Secretary-General.)

The putschist leaders informed the world through their message to the UN that the banner of perestroika which had fallen from the weakened hands of Gorbachev was held firmly by reformers from the State of Emergency Committee. However, virtually all Western leaders, as well as the EEC leadership, unanimously condemned the coup which took place on August 19. The putschists' actions were defined as unconstitutional. On August 20, a meeting of the EEC Foreign Ministers discussed the situation in the USSR and froze the program of the EEC's large-scale assistance to the Soviet Union. Almost all those who granted this aid in the past suspended it.

The State of Emergency Committee appealed to the UN and presented the coup to the world community as a fait accompli. By their appeal the putschists wanted to justify the "unusual" way, whereby they had attained power.

However, this venture had an unexpected result. Only two people, namely Muammar al-Gaddafi, the leader of the Libyan revolution, and Saddam Hussein, the "hero" of the war in the Gulf, recognized the State of Emergency Committee. Gaddafi even said that the coup had been "well done." Hussein expressed the hope that thanks to the coup "we would restore the balance of forces in the world."

The first reports from news agencies indicated that the UN did not recognize "the country of the State of Emergency Committee." China was the only member of the Security Council to reserve judgement under the pretext of non-interference in our internal affairs. On August 20th US President George Bush not only refused to recognize the State of Emergency Committee, as his statement distributed by the White House infers, but demanded that the legitimate President of the USSR be reestablished in power. If this was not done, the USA threatened to revoke through Congress the Soviet-American trade agreement. British Prime Minister John Major, President of France Francois Mitterrand, West German Chancellor Helmut Kohl, Japanese Prime Minister Toshiki Kaifu, Spanish Prime Minister Felipe Gonzalez, the leaders of Scandinavian and other European countries, ASEAN and Mexico resolutely condemned the putschists.

The West did not confine itself to statements and supported President Bush's appeal to freeze the programs of assistance to the USSR. Britain froze 85 million dollars of technical assistance to the USSR. Spain suspended credits worth almost one billion dollars, Australia 390 million and Japan 100 million dollars. On August 20th the EEC Foreign Ministers, when discussing the situation in the USSR, also resolved to interrupt the programs of the EEC's assistance to the USSR to a total amount of 945 million dollars. A U.S. Congressional Committee voiced its intention to exercise a strict control over the supplies of American agricultural products to the USSR.

As proof of international support for the legitimate government of the USSR, employees of foreign embassies in Moscow are maintaining regular contacts with the Russian Government. On August 20th, Russian President Boris Yeltsin was visited by representatives of the U.S. and German Embassies. After receiving the letter from Yeltsin, wherein he analyzed the situation in the USSR, President Bush contacted him by phone, expressing support for his struggle and emphasizing that the U.S. would not maintain normal relations with people who had gained power by unlawful means. As a result of these contacts, Russian Foreign Minister Andrei Kozyrev left on a tour of Western countries, beginning in Paris on August 20th.

The East European countries, which had faced similar situations in the recent past were especially concerned about the military coup in the USSR. The leaders of Poland, Czechoslovakia, Hungary and Bulgaria held emergency meetings with the ministers of foreign affairs, defense and the interior, and resolved to fortify their eastern borders.

Thus, to the great astonishment of the putschists, the world community rejected the so-called "saviours of the country," considering them to be common criminals.

THE PUTSCHISTS—WHO WERE THEY?

The past determines the future. The biographies and political stands of the members of the State Committee for the State of Emergency will help to form a picture of life in the country in the event the putsch had turned out to be successful.

Boris Pugo,

Minister of the Interior

Born in 1937 in Kalinin. From 1961 to 1976 was a Komsomol and party functionary in Riga. Since 1976 had worked in state security bodies. In 1980 he became head of the KGB in Latvia, and in 1984, first secretary of the Central Committee of the Communist Party of Latvia. When reformist forces began to gain in strength in the Latvian Communist Party in 1987, was transferred to the CPSU Central Committee shortly before the Plenary Meeting of the Latvian Central Committee. In 1988 he became Chairman of the Party Control Committee under the CPSU Central Committee. After Vadim Bakatin's resignation, was appointed Minister of the Interior of the USSR.

One of Pugo's first steps in the capacity of minister was to introduce joint patrolling by militia and troops.

Boris Pugo first demanded that the state of emergency be introduced in the country at a USSR Supreme Soviet session in June this year, shortly before Russian Presidential elections. The demand to introduce the state of emergency was made at the same meeting by Defense Minister Yazov and KGB Chairman Kryuchkov.

When departization of the Armenian population was prepared in Azerbaijan, Pugo ordered the withdrawal of the troops of the interior from Armenian villages, so that the 4th army and the republican OMON forces would have a free hand there; after that he declared: "Interior ministry troops are not taking part in the events in Karabakh."

During the pogroms of the Lithuanian customs posts, Pugo declared: "I know nothing about the people who carried out the assaults." And only after the TV report by Leningrad journalist Nevzorov concerning the participation of OMON troops from Vilnius, which are directly subordinated to Moscow, he ordered that an official investigation be carried out. The results of the investigation are still unknown, but starting in June, Pugo again declared that he had heard nothing about the pogroms by OMON troops.

Gennady Yanayev,

Vice-President of the USSR

At the end of 1990 the President of the USSR managed only after two attempts to put Gennady Yanayev in the post of Vice-President. Thereby Gorbachev had evidently decided to act on his promise to "transform the leadership by appointing the best representatives of society."

Gennady Yanayev is 53, an engineer; graduated from the correspondence department of a law institute, holds the title of candidate of historical sciences; his thesis is devoted to anachronisms and trotskyism. Began his political career by working as a Komsomol functionary; was responsible for "relations with foreign youth unions," including in the capacity of chairman of the Committee of Youth Organization of the USSR. From there he made a smooth transition to posts that were again connected with promoting friendship with foreign countries: vice-chairman of the Presidium of the Union of Soviet Societies of Friendship and Cultural Relations; then Secretary and Chairman of the AUCCTU. In 1990 moved over to the building of the CPSU Central Committee in Staraya Poloshchad, becoming Secretary of the CPSU Central Committee. At the 4th Congress of People's Deputies of the USSR he headed the faction of communists. "I am proud of being a member of the CPSU Central Committee," he declared at the press-conference on August 19.

Yanayev's position at the roll-call voting in parliament was as follows: he was against the president submitting an income declaration, against the president making an annual report to Congress and against adopting a declaration on the sovereignty of the republics.

Gennady Yanayev is also known for having replied at the Congress to a question about his health: "My wife has nothing to complain about."

Oleg Baklanov,

First Deputy Chairman of the USSR Defense Council.

Born in Kharkov in 1932. Began his working career as an assemblyman. Joined the CPSU in 1953. In 1958 graduated from the USSR Correspondence Power Institute, holds title of candidate of technical sciences. Has risen all the way to general director of a defense production association. In 1976 became deputy, then first deputy, and in April 1983 Minister of General Machine-Building.

From 1986 member of the CPSU Central Committee, and from February 1988 to April 1991 Secretary of the CPSU Central Committee. Was in charge of the military-industrial complex, became known as an opponent of conversion, which he characterized as a severe blow to the defense industry. People's Deputy of the USSR from the CPSU. Hero of Socialist Labor, has received six orders, medals and one Lenin Prize.

During the penultimate discussion of the Union Treaty in Novo-Ogaryovo, he advanced his own project which was strongly opposed by Nursultan Nazarbayev. Baklanov considers "the preservation of the USSR as a single great power with sovereign development as the basic national interest of the USSR and all nations and nationalities it incorporates."

As long ago as last May Baklanov spoke of the possibility of the transfer of power to the army in "post-perestroika" conditions. It "will have to take upon itself management of the economy, transport and society as a whole." Baklanov believes that the army "will be able only for some time to maintain such management, and even that at an extremely low level. The army will be interested in transferring management to civilians as soon as possible and promoting the restoration of civilian structures." (Den., 9.04.91).

Vasily Starodubtsev,

Chairman of the Farmers' Union of the USSR

Born in 1931, graduated from the All-Union Correspondence Agricultural Institute. In 1963 became collective farm chairman in Novomoskovskoye village. Starodubtsev was considered as one of the initiators of large-size agricultural entities and was one of the first to organize an agro-industrial association. Initially, he was restricted, but then he was supported by journalists as much as that was possible in conditions of stagnation. Then all problems with the higher-ups were eliminated. In 1976 he was awarded the Gold Star of a Hero of Labor and became winner of the 1979 State Prize. The farm he headed became a model setting an example for socialist farming.

With the launching of the perestroika drive Starodubtsev began to conduct active publicist work. Many national newspapers regularly printed his interviews, in which he stressed most often: "Enough giving orders, let's start working" censuring the existing agro-industrial structures for being bureaucratic. In 1988 he became corresponding member of the National Agricultural Academy named after Lenin.

The tone of his numerous speeches changed after the appearance of the first signs of non-collective farming. He did not approve of individual farming. Typical are the following publications he made at the close of 1990: "I am against extreme measures" (Selskaya Zhizn, 17.10.90), "Do not Impose your Will" (Sovetskaya Rossia, 30.11.90), "We are concerned for the thesis about buying and selling land, private ownership of land for agricultural production. Today, the peasant is not what he used to be..." In April 1990 Starodubtsev was elected chairman of the Union of Agrarians of the Russian Federation. Before the new organization could produce anything tangible, a new one was set up in June---the Farmers' Union of the USSR. Of its 1,817 delegates only six represented agricultural cooperators and 120, peasant economies. The rest were managers. A 120-man strong Central Council of the Union was elected, with the quota for peasants and lease-holders set at eight people.

Valentin Pavlov,

Prime Minister of the USSR

Born on September 26, 1937. Graduated from the Moscow Financial Economics Institute; began his working career as a revenue inspector.

Became CPSU member in 1962; appeared on the political arena in 1989 as Minister of Finance of the USSR. The taxation law which the Supreme Soviet of the USSR adopted in 1990 is connected with Pavlov's name. He is the author of the book "On Taxes on the Population" (M. 1990). Has made repeated statements on his allegiance to the principle of collective leadership. As for his political credo, he has time and again declared it in the mass media and demonstrated it by his actions: right after he was officially endorsed as prime minister, Valentin Pavlov emphatically assured the population that there would be no money reform in the visible future. His deputies swore that there would not be an exchange of bank notes. However a few days later, a wholesale change of 50- and 100-rouble bank notes was carried out in the country. Soon after that the prime-minister said the following commenting on the necessity of that step: "A mass injection of money into the country has been in preparation for a long time. This is being done by various means, including the buying up of 100- and 50- rouble notes. Banking organizations in our country have joined in this action, and so have a number of private banks in Austria, Switzerland and Canada...Such actions were carried out in many regions of the world when they wanted to change the political system and to overthrow unsuitable political figures. The president was simply in someone's way... We had to run against time. It will be up to history to evaluate the rest..."

Pavlov described his relations with the country's president as "good" and "businesslike." Valentin Pavlov said the following about the role of the party in modern society: "No matter how loudly the party's opponents mourn the party, no matter how hard they try to crowd it out of political life... the party has been and remains the country's most influential and capable force."

On June 17 the Prime Minister demanded from the Supreme Soviet of the USSR extraordinary powers for the Cabinet of Ministers, including legislative initiative; he proposed that a state of emergency be immediately introduced in transport, in branches of the fuel and energy complex and metallurgy. If necessary, admitted Pavlov, a state of emergency could be introduced also in some regions of the country.

According to confidential information, Valentin Sergeyevich has always been quick to react to changes in the political situation. Thus on the morning of August 20 he experienced a crisis of hypertension and spent the whole day in bed.

Vladimir Kryuchkov, Chairman of the State Security Committee of the USSR (KGB),

Born 1924; educated at the National Law Institute and Foreign Ministry Higher Diplomatic School; member of the Communist Party of the Soviet Union since 1944; CPSU Central Committee Politburo member.

Vladimir Kryuchkov began to work as a marker at a defense plant in Volgograd (Stalingrad) during the Second World War and was then elected a Komsomol organizer at the YCL Central Committee. Later on he worked as secretary of a district Komsomol committee and enrolled in the Saratov Institute of Law. In 1946--1947 he worked as an investigator at the prosecutor's office and in 1947--1951 as a prosecutor. Well-informed sources in the central apparatus of the KGB claim that Kryuchkov strongly opposed the establishment of a memorial to the victims of the GULAG in Lubyanka Square.

After finishing diplomatic school, Kryuchkov was sent to Hungary as third secretary of the Soviet Embassy in Budapest (1955--1959). There is reason to believe that he met Yuri Andropov there, who he worked under for many years.

In 1959 Kryuchkov was appointed to the Central Committee apparatus, where he worked first as a consultant and then as sector head of a department, and assistant to a Central Committee secretary.

In 1967 he was transferred to the KGB and became its chief on Gorbachev's initiative in 1988.

At the fourth congress of people's deputies of the USSR, Kryuchkov devoted his speech to "destructive political forces" and "the struggle against economic sabotage." Less than a month later, on January 23, 1991, he made the following comment on the tragic events in Vilnius in an interview for the weekly Literaturnaya Gazeta: "No one denies Lithuania its right to secede from the USSR... But that should be done in accordance with the law."

When asked whether there was a conspiracy to overthrow the legal government of Lithuania or some other region of the country, Kryuchkov said: "We had no information indicating that someone was plotting such a conspiracy... Under our laws the use of force to forcibly overthrow the existing system, even of the public calls for such actions, are indictable crimes."

In a speech delivered at a closed meeting of the Soviet legislature, the Supreme Soviet, on June 18, 1991, Kryuchkov supported Prime Minister Valentin Pavlov's demand that the Cabinet of Ministers be granted emergency powers.

Dmitry Yazov, Minister of Defense of the USSR,

Dmitry Timofeyevich Yazov was born in the village of Yazovo, in the Omsk Region in 1923. He fought in the Second World War and subsequently set his heart on becoming a professional military soldier. He commanded the Far Eastern military district and was deputy minister of defense.

When Mathias Rust landed his plane in the Red Square, Defense Minister Sergei Sokolov was dismissed from his post and Yazov took over.

In December 1990 the leaders of the KGB, the Interior Ministry and the Soviet Army issued a statement saying that weapons would be used "without firing warning shots" should any military town be attacked and added that the army would have military garrisons in all republics "wherever it considers that necessary."

On democrats, Yazov once said: "I don't understand who are democrats and who are conservatives. Those who advocate socialist positions and want to preserve the Soviet Union are called conservatives and those who want to divide this country into many states and break up the army are called democrats."

Addressing a meeting of military members of parliament, Yazov thanked them for being faithful to Party traditions and principles: "You have not surrendered to the government of Russia. Thank you very much... We are so scared by the Tbilisi syndrome that we have gone into hiding. We hate private property and this unites us. We are patriots and must be united."

On November 12, 1990, Yazov met Gorbachev and bluntly told him that "it is time to stop the rise of nationalism and extremism."

On January 1, 1991, when a correspondent of the weekly Moscow News asked him whether the army was going to interfere in politics, Yazov said that it was and in June 1991 he was one of the three leaders who demanded that the national legislature impose a state of emergency, but received rebuff from President Gorbachev.

On the night of August 20 to 21 rumors about Yazov's resignation appeared but were never confirmed.

Alexander Tizyakov, President of the Association of State Enterprises and Industrial, Construction, Transport and Communications Associations,

Born in 1926; fought in the Second World War; has several war medals and orders; educated at the Urals Polytechnic; holder of a Ph.D. in economics.

He began to work in 1950 as a driver. In 1956 he was employed as a technician at the "Kalinin Machine-Building Plant" research and production association in Sverdlovsk and later worked as the association's communist party committee secretary and chief engineer. Tizyakov is currently general director of the association and Vice-President of the Scientific and Industrial Union of the USSR.

A biographical note about Tizyakov, prepared for a national plant managers' conference, said that his main quality of a political leader was "a desire to use the positive experience of state enterprises in the transition to a market-based economy."

Tizyakov repeatedly emphasized that his association represented virtually all factory and plant managers in the country. But it can hardly represent the interests of all plant managers of the USSR because it is mainly composed of representatives of the military-industrial complex. Most other factory and plant managers were members of the Association of Plant Managers of the USSR and other associations.

On December 6 and 7 last year the Association of State Enterprises held a national conference. The report made at that conference by Tizyakov was, in effect, an ultimatum from the military-industrial complex to the President of the USSR. Tizyakov demanded a ban on strikes, the preservation of old ministerial structures and the suspension of reforms in the basic industries.

Gorbachev reportedly reacted to that report with the following remark: "You are trying to scare me. I shall not be scared." Experts believe that Gorbachev's rebuttal to the ultimatum made Tizyakov join the organizers of the coup.

Vladimir Denisenko, the communist party city committee worker in Sverdlovsk, described Tizyakov as "one of the few real Bolsheviks," while workers at the Kalinin Machine-Building Plant claim that their manager was hard, straightforward and a passionate hunter.

People who know Tizyakov well say that he shared many of the views of former Prime Minister Valentin Pavlov's adviser Sergei Kurginyan, co-author of the book "Post-Perestroika" and chief ideologist for the restoration of a communist state.

Tizyakov was one of the 12 "patriots" who signed the notorious "Appeal to the Nation." If the coup had succeeded, he would have been made prime minister.

Yazov: 10 Minutes for the Coup. The Countdown begins

A. Krainy

A meeting in Dmitry Yazov's office began at 6:00 a.m. on August 19. The minister made a 10-minute statement. He instructed the military district commanders to maintain law and order and, depending on the situation, enhance the protection of military facilities (conventional and nuclear ammunition depots). The defense minister also urged military commanders not to yield to provocation. "You will learn everything else from radio broadcasts," he concluded.

Consequently the overwhelming majority of those present at the meeting (the entire military leadership) knew nothing. The acting commander of the ground forces, Col.-Gen. S. Kolesnikov confirms this: "The defense minister's report came as a complete surprise to me, but I knew that troops should unquestionably obey any order. I'm now receiving reports from district commanders. They have reported from Siberia, the Lake Baikal region, the Far East, Central Asia and Azerbaijan that the situation is calm there and there are no violations of law. The same is true of a large part of the Ukraine. Although we are watching closely the situation in the Transcaucasus, no alarming reports have emerged from there. Unrest is possible in Moscow and consequently troops have been brought into the city."

It should be noted that the units of the Taman motorized rifle division and the Kantemir tank division entering the city were involved in similar events in the past. They were alerted when Beria (Stalin's right-hand man) was arrested and When Khrushchev was on holiday in the Black Sea resort town of Pitsunda.

UNITED NEWSPAPER: WILL GORBACHEV LEAVE THE CPSU

By Ye. Krasnikov

On August 19, the 11 newspapers banned by the self-styled Soviet government, acting under the name of the State Emergency Committee, decided to ignore its Order No. 1. Those newspapers valued above all the first provision of the law on the Press: censorship in the mass media is inadmissible.

How could they become accomplices to fraud? The 11 insurgent newspapers preferred to die standing rather than live in an abject fawning state, as demonstrated by the traditional Communist press. On August 20, Russia's Ministry for the Press and Information registered the *Obshchaya Gazeta* (United Newspaper), to be issued underground for the next several months.

But happily it lived for only one day because the junta, which had yearned to swallow up the press, ended up choking on it.

The eleven newspapers stood firm before the tanks, the formidable decrees and other emergency items of the Emergency Committee.

The word proved to be more powerful than the bullet. The words were uttered by journalists from "Argumenty I Fakty," "Kuranty," "Commersant," "Komsomolskaya Pravda," "Megapolis-Express," "Moscow News," "Nezavisimaya Gazeta," "Rossiyskaya Gazeta," "Rossiyskiye Vesti" and the magazine "Stolitsa."

The truth has helped us save democracy and freedom. We are happy that the *United Newspaper* died shortly after its birth and that subscribers will be able to receive the disobedient periodicals as they did before August 19.

We should confess that we were scared too. Perhaps even more than our readers who kept phoning us and offering help during those days.

Thank you very much!

Thank you, dear colleagues, who were off the list of authorized journalists and contributed to our efforts during all those alarming hours of the coup. Paradoxically, but we never felt as free as we did during the putsch.

Farewell to our *United Newspaper*! Readers, subscribe to the newspapers and magazines which the putschists tried to strike off the catalogue of periodicals.

WE HAVE WON: WHAT HAPPENED TO GORBACHEV?

In the evening of August 20th Sergei Stankevich, acting Chairman of the Mossovet (Moscow City Soviet), gave his version of the operation to confine Mikhail Gorbachev to his summer house at Cape Foros in the Crimea.

Stankevich's version is confirmed by the bits of information which keep coming to our paper. The following is an abridged text of Stankevich's report.

We have at our disposal the following information about what happened at President Gorbachev's house at Cape Foros on August 19.

At 04:00 hours two tractors blocked the runway at Bilbek airfield, near Cape Foros, where President Gorbachev's Tu-134 plane and Mi-08 helicopter were stationed. This was done on orders from Colonel-General Maltsev, chief of the headquarters of the air-defense troops of the USSR. The action was carried through by the Sevastopol regiment of the KGB troops. The regiment currently controls the President's house. At 10:42 there were attempts to remove the plane and the helicopter from the airfield.

Then followed orders from General Yasinsky to use the plane for removing nine servicemen. However, the servicemen were not available. The plane stood waiting till 18:43. At 18:43, on orders from Colonel-General Denisov, chief of the General Staff's operations department, permission was granted to use the plane for transporting the following persons: Kozlov, Gubernatorov, Alexandrova and Sorokina. Gubernatorov is one of Gorbachev's bodyguards, and Alexandrova and Sorokina are his personal secretaries. KGB officers checked the documents of all these people. At 19:38 the plane took off and headed for Vnukovo. The President's communications means were also on board.

The Presidential helicopter was forced to fly to Simferopol at 21:00 hours.

A complete air and sea blockade is in effect south of the President's house. Up to 16 ships lie in the roadstead east of Cape Foros.

Beginning at 16:00 hrs. on August 19th no planes, ships and cars are being allowed near the Cape Foros house.

At 14:30 hrs. it was reported from Moscow that the large residential plane which Gorbachev had ordered would not arrive. Gorbachev ordered this plane two days earlier to go to Moscow on August 19.

At 15:10 hrs. on August 19 General Maltsev gave his first oral order. Here is its text" "Some people from the former President's inner circle attempted to get to Gorbachev. If similar attempts are repeated, I order that the persons who commit them should be detained and handed over to the KGB bodies."

According to unconfirmed information, an attempt to get to the President was made by Shakhnazarov, one of his assistants. Kept at the Cape Foros house together with the President are: General Vladimir Medvedev, chief of the President's bodyguards, Anatoli Chernyaev and Georgi Shakhnazarov, the President's assistants. Shakhnazarov's family: his wife Anna and his son Karen, a famous film director---are also there. The Shakhnazarov family stayed at the Yuzhny holiday home near Cape Foros.

Thus, immediate witnesses of the developments are ready to confirm the information which I have given you. It is perfectly clear that we have a case of a forceful ouster from power of a legitimate President and his forceful detention. A very grave crime against the state has therefore been committed. All persons who are in one way or another involved in this crime as well as those who in any way assist the development of this anti-government conspiracy also commit a crime and will have to answer before the law.

"In this connection I would like to appeal to all servicemen and officers of the Interior Ministry and the KGB. Do not make a fatal mistake by shedding the blood of your brothers and sisters, for you will have the curse of your country and posterity."

No. 35, 1991

PRESIDENTIAL COMMUNICATIONS BREAKDOWN: REAL OR IMAGINARY?

For Gorbachev the August coup began when he realized that his telephones were dead. Now, when a handful of plotters have the power to instantly switch off one of the most important communications networks in this country what's the point of the network and of the security system protecting it? However, opinions vary on this issue.

The "Moscow News" has received a letter from Director General of Leningrad-based Signal industrial group Valentin Zanin. The letter says, "Having read Gorbachev's version of the events as reported by the press I insist that the USSR President cannot be isolated from his communications facilities in such a manner. I am one of the producers of various communications systems, and if the President hasn't been physically removed or handicapped to isolate him from his communications system requires physical dismantling, confiscation and removal of the equipment. It is clear from the report that this wasn't done. The equipment weigh many tons. We are dealing with the fact that the President made a conscious choice not to establish contact... (signed, August 24, 1991, Zanin."

Valentin Zanin supplied a verbal note to his information, "You must realize that it's not just a matter of this country house. This is one of the key points from which he can control the country, and it houses numerous mutually independent communications systems. If the electricity is switched off a local generator will be activated. If that breaks down they can use a battery. If the battery goes wrong there is a manual device. When this cannot be done there is yet another communications system which I cannot speak about. All the President needed to do was to pick up a pen and a sheet of paper in order to establish contact with the rest of the country.

Are we dealing with an attempt to whitewash the producer's good name or the deliberate isolation of the President from his communications facilities? An answer can only be provided by an investigation. By the way, there are other opinions with regard to this.

"It is possible to switch off the communications units in Mikhail Gorbachev's country house in the Crimea," Chief of the 8th Department of the USSR KGB Nikolai Andreyev has told a "Moscow News" correspondent.

According to him, in spite of the vast amount of equipment used to maintain normal operation of the communications system it is fairly easy to disengage the telephones in the President's office in Foros.

"Moscow News" doesn't subscribe to either opinion but considers it necessary to publish this important information.

"Moscow News" has shown the document to Anatoly Chernyayev, an aide to the USSR President. Chernyayev said that he was familiar with the document and had shown it to Gorbachev. He views the entire matter as a blatant nonsense, because all the communications were cut off. The fact is that according to Gorbachev, all these new versions are being suggested by the same forces that at first sought to get rid of the President and are now trying to discredit him at any cost.

Chernyayev shares the President's point of view, saying, "Rumors are going to crawl out of very corner. Gorbachev has made a move with regard to the CPSU. He has severed the umbilical cord, a decision which took him a long time to make. This has antagonized many people who will be attending the forthcoming congress and the session currently under way."

Chernyayev has said that, according to a statement made by General Gheneralov, on the evening of August 19 a military airplane removed the special communications systems and operators from the Crimea.

Chernyayev has expressed his regret that footage was censored from the Vzglyad show broadcast by the Central Television Network on August 25 which spoke about the moral pressure brought on the plotters under investigation to convince them that they were just ordinary criminals.

WE HAD ONLY THIRTY MINUTES... GORBACHEV'S TELEPHONE CALL TO LT. SKORODUMOV

By Alexander Fedorov

Main Characters:

Generals of the Defense Ministry and the General Staff;

Senior Lieutenant Igor Skorodumov, a member of the staff of the General Staff's Eighty Directorate; Warrant-Officer Grigory Stepanov, a programmer at the General Staff Hospital; President Gorbachev.

A Chronicle of Events. August 22nd, 10 a.m. A General Staff department for the elimination of secret documents receives an order to burn official correspondence and coded telegrams received and dispatched from August 19th to 21st. The order is received by Senior Lieutenant Skorodumov.

At 10:10 a.m. Skorodumov calls his friend, Grigory Stepanov, a programmer at the General Staff Hospital, who is in charge of a computer network not controlled by military channels. It becomes known that 14 telegrams have been destroyed.

At 10:15 Stepnaov contacts a programmer friend in the Soviet Academy of Sciences through an electronic communications system and asks him to pass on this information to any member of parliament.

At 10:30 hours Yegor Yakovlev, an MP and editor of the weekly Moscow News, asks for confirmation of the information received by his newspaper. After that he contacts Russian Federation Secretary of State Gennady Burbulis. The Russian President's Staff takes measures. Meanwhile, Stepanov's assistant manages to put a call through to Gorbachev's reception-room.

At 11:00 hours Mikhail Gorbachev calls Senior Lieutenant Skorodumov by city telephone and as Supreme Commander orders him not to destroy any documents, ensure the protection of the entire archives by officers, keep that secret and report further developments to his aides.

Testimony. "I, Senior Lieutenant Skorodumov, consider it my duty to report on some of the actions of the Defense Ministry leadership during the period of August 19 to 21. These data are in the fourth department of the

Eighth Directorate of the General Staff, the code department. Coded communications are used exclusively for the transmission of the most important documents, each copy of which is strictly controlled, checked and tracked until it is destroyed or transferred to the archives. At the moment the fourth department keeps all coded telegrams the General Staff leadership has received from the Defense Ministry containing resolutions and decisions and signatures of individual officials. Most of the telegrams reveal the senders' attitude to the coup. I am convinced that an attempt has been made to destroy some of the coded telegrams signed by individual officials. If this happens, they will be able to claim that they knew nothing about this information and, consequently, bear no legal responsibility. Here is just one excerpt from a telegram signed by army General Varennikov: "Any delay may be fatal. Haven't we agreed Yeltsin should be the first to be arrested?"

Warrant-Officer Stepanov: "As far as I know, the military organizers of the coup began to act at 4:30 a.m. on August 19. In fact, the conspirators were active for more than three days. The order to destroy the documents came on August 22, that is when Gorbachev was already in Moscow and some of the coup leaders had been arrested. I don't know now how this all would have ended if we had no computer communications and what would have happened if we had failed to contact Yakovlev and through him Yeltsin. We had only thirty minutes."

A Kind of Epilogue. A special commission is working in the General Staff, which will not only analyze the orders and messages of the early days of the coup but also find out who gave the order to destroy this correspondence.

P.S. On August 26, Mikhail Gorbachev met Yegor Yakovlev and asked him to thank through his paper Senior Lieutenant Igor Skorodumov.

(Moscow News No. 35, 1991)

ALL THE WAY TO CAPE FOROS AND BACK—WITH THE PRESIDENT

By Alexander Budberg

Interviews Alexander Korovnikov, Chairman of a Committee of the RSFSR Supreme Soviet

Question: How was the trip to Cape Foros planned?
Answer: One of our concerns during the coup was the fate of Mikhail Gorbachev. Somebody spread rumors on August 19 that the President had been killed in a skirmish. There were rumors that he had been airlifted to Moscow and that his plane had landed at Vnukovo Airport. We did not know where Gorbachev was or what had happened to him. So when the MPs unanimously banned Boris Yeltsin from flying to the Crimea, as proposed by Kryuchkov, Ivan Silayev stood up and suggested that he and Rutskoy (Vice-President of Russia) should go there. A group of MPs was to accompany them.

We had to get ready within seconds. We were supposed to carry arms, but I had no time to go to my office and take my Kalashnikov (assault rifle).
Question: When did you take off?
Answer: Minutes after four o'clock. Before that, however, we were informed that a convoy of government ZIL limousines carrying Yazov and Kryuchkov was heading for Vnukovo Airport. At 2:15 p.m. they left Moscow for the Crimea aboard the presidential airplane. The news gave rise to utmost concern, but at least we knew that Gorbachev was alive.

We were accompanied by Silayev's and Rutskoy's guards and personnel of the Ryazan Interior Ministry Academy. They formed a task force which was to be used in case of skirmishes. In all, 54 people were on board.

When we arrived at Vunkovo, the task force was already there, standing by our plane.
Question: What kind of a plane was it?
Answer: It was Yeltsin's Tupolev-134.
Question: Did you have any difficulty landing?
Answer: There were three options. We were to land either at Bilbek Air Force field, the Simferopol airport or the Sevastopol airport. Bilbek was

clearly the best choice as the distance from the airfield to the residence is a mere 60 kilometers, but air force controllers did not allow us to land. It was then that Rutskoy suggested switching on the emergency lights and trying to land at Bilbek. According to standing regulations, the runway should be cleared of all planes and motor vehicles in such cases.

We consulted Yeltsin. He said we should land in Simferopol. Cars were waiting for us there, and local law enforcement agencies were informed about our arrival.

Suddenly, when we were approaching the Crimea, Bilbek gave us permission to land. That was good, but we felt ill at ease. We though that it could be one Kryuchkov's tricks and that we would be met by KGB special operations troops upon landing. We started making plans for disembarkation.

Question: Why did Bilbek suddenly give you permission to land?

Answer: Today we know that by that time Gorbachev's communications had been restored and he had assisted in arranging our landing at Bilbek.

When we landed, our plane was ordered to stop at the edge of the runway far from all structures. In general, the place was right for an attack against us. But, on the other hand, everything seemed quiet.

We decided to disembark in the following order: first went Silayev's and Rutskoy's bodyguards, they were followed by Russia's vice-president and prime minister, MPs, Bakatin and Primakov. The task force was ready to give us fire support, although as a military man I knew that in case of an attack we could have held out for only about ten--fifteen minutes.

Question: Were there any cars waiting for you?

Answer: Only two Volga cars and an UAZ Jeep. True, we were told that several more cars dispatched by the Black Sea command would arrive soon. There was not time to lose so we drove off at once. The French minister joined us.

Question: How was the President's dacha guarded?

Answer: When we arrived there, the perimeter was already guarded by the President's security detail.

We tried to pass one checkpoint but were told to go away. When we approached the main entrance I saw tarpaulined army trucks leaving the place. It was dark and I could not see who was in the trucks.

Gorbachev's guards said afterwards the place had been blocked by their comrades-in-arms, KGB special operations troops. For three days they faced each other with weapons at the ready.

Question: What happened after you passed the checkpoint?

Answer: Our cars were stopped. Only eight people were allowed inside: Silayev, Rutskoy, MPs Sergeyev and Stolyarov, myself, Bakatin, Primakov and Russia's Justice Minister Fedorof.

We saw four Volga cars. We drove on for maybe another twenty meters and approached the first building. Its porch was dimly lit and we saw

Yazov and Kryuchkov standing there. We went out and walked down the road to the dacha. At one point we were at a distance of five meters from the two men.

We were led into the living room. Gorbachev joined as in several minutes. He hugged all of us and said he knew we were coming and had been looking forward to seeing us.

We talked for about one hour. Gorbachev answered our main question at once when he told us that he considered the whole thing to be a military coup d'etat. He told us what had happened on Cape Foros during those three days. We informed him about the developments in Moscow and told him what we thought of those who had betrayed him. We discussed Lukyanov's role. Everyone agreed that he was the main ideologist of the coup.

Then we began to discuss the tactics of our return trip. The president wanted to use his own liner but we talked him out of it, because Kryuchkov had not fully lost his control over the KGB. As for our plane, it was guarded and the crew was highly reliable. Gorbachev agreed. We compiled lists of persons who were to accompany the president on his flight to Moscow: his family, assistants and bodyguards. In all, the lists included 38 people. Now, since Tupolev-134 is not so big, we could not take all of them on board.

Rutskoy and I went to Bilbek to arrange the departure. When we walked out of the dacha—it was already dark—we bumped into Lukyanov and Ivashko who were on their way to Gorbachev. We stopped on front of each other in silence that was rather embarrassing. Lukyanov stretched out his hand toward Rutskoy and said: "Hello, Sasha." Rutskoy shook his hand. Ivashko, who stood behind Lukyanov's back, also greeted us. We stood facing each other. The pause was awkward. Then Alexander Vladimirovich (Rutskoy) turned away and raced toward the car.

Question: How did you arrange the flight back?

Answer: First of all, we cordoned off the ZIL limousine which Yazov and Kryuchkov were using: such limos are equipped with telecommunications systems including satellite-aided ones. We did so to prevent the conspirators from issuing any orders. We also ensure that the telecommunications of the big presidential liner could not be used for that purpose.

Soon Gorbachev arrived. He stopped briefly near his plane, giving orders to the captain and chief of the security detail, and then proceeded toward our plane.

Kryuchkov was told to board our plane. We said Gorbachev asked him to do so.

Question: How did Kryuchkov's and Yazov's bodyguards react to what was happening?

Answer: I'm not sure about Yazov's bodyguards, but Kryuchkov was accompanied by eight people. They were cordoned off and later arrived in Moscow on board the presidential plane.

Question: What was Kryuchkov's reaction like?

Answer: He was calm. He sat by the window. He sank back in the chair and closed his eyes. He was silent all the way back to Moscow. When we touched down everyone walked out and only Kryuchkov, one of Silayev's bodyguards and myself remained in the plane. He turned to us and asked: "Am I under arrest?" We did not answer. In went Dunayev, Russia's deputy interior minister and told us that we could escort Kryuchkov out of the plane. We accompanied him down the landing ramp in the back. A minibus was waiting on the tarmac and it took Kryuchkov to a specially prepared place not far from Moscow.

Question: Who guarded the perimeter of Vnukovo-2?

Answer: Operatives from Russia's interior ministry.

Question: Did the president go home at once?

Answer: Yes, he did.

WHAT KIND OF A PLANE DOES THE PRESIDENT HAVE?

The activities of heads of state are usually shrouded in secrecy, and this is quite understandable. Still some people would like to know what aircraft does the USSR President use. Information is scarce; however, we have managed to piece together information from various sources. And here's what we have found out.

First. Five top national executives have the right to use "private" aircraft so far. They are as follows---USSR President, USSR Vice-President, Chairman of the USSR Supreme Soviet, USSR Prime Minister and USSR Foreign Minister. In the past when there were so many Politburo members, even more bigwigs could fly aboard special planes. Still even they couldn't use Presidential aircraft, which are equipped with special communications units. These include the following aircraft types---two Ilyushin Il-62M airliners, two Tupolefv Tu-154 jets, two Tu-134s, two Yakovlev Yak-40 jetliners and several helicopter models. These planes resemble conventional aircraft in appearance. An Il-62M consists of a Presidential compartment replete with a bedroom featuring two sofas, a study featuring a table and two arm-chairs. Apart from that, the plane features a small conference room with a corner sofa and table, as well as a communications room, a snack bar and a kitchen, 8 arm-chairs and tables that are reserved for aides and 30 conventional seats.

Other aircraft have a similar layout; however, as distinct from the Il-62M, any of the two Tu-154s features a Presidential compartment in its front section.

Second. Here's how any Presidential liner was used. A KGB security chief would phone the Civil Aviation Ministry, reporting the time of departure and type of plane to its officials. After that, the Civil Aviation Ministry would send coded messages to all main air force and air-defense headquarters, warning them that the Presidential plane was ready to take off. This procedure used to take some 4 to 5 hours. And if the President was flying abroad, Soviet ambassadors stationed in respective countries were notified, as well. For their part, they had to notify competent local services. Government aircraft streak along the same, preset, routes and corridors as conventional planes do. However, special corridors have been set aside for "executive" planes leaving the Moscow sector, with the afore-said planes enjoying the right of the road here. Chief of the former No. 235 separate aircraft detachment and KGB security chief used to fly aboard the Presidential aircraft not so long ago.

The detachment employs top-notch civilian pilots. In fact, the USSR is the only country whose governments are transported by civilian crews.

Third. By all looks. the putschists failed to escape elsewhere aboard a Presidential plane. Still, they might have succeeded, who knows...At any rate, they had enough time to get a ride on this liner...

(Komsomolskaya Pravda, August 31, 1991)

PRESIDENT GORBACHEV MEETS WITH RUSSIAN PARLIAMENTARIANS

Mikhail Gorbachev met with Russian Parliamentarians at the "White House," the seat of the Russian Parliament, in Moscow's Krasnopresnenskaya Embankment on August 23rd.

The opening speech was made by Russian President Boris Yeltsin. He congratulated Russian legislators on the "victory over the reactionary forces, the organizers of the putsch, the coup."

The Russian President announced that all participants in the coup had been arrested and would face trial.

Yeltsin said that they discussed personnel problems today with President Gorbachev and later with the Nine. Most of the personnel problems were resolved.

Gorbachev addressed people's deputies of the Russian Federation:

I will begin with the things which I have already tried to say in the past few days. Thinking over what has happened and appraising what each has been doing, I want to pay tribute to the position assumed by the Russian Federation.

First of all the Russian people in their mass, the Russian Parliament, which expressed the will and interests of the Russian people, the government of the Russian Federation rallied and barred the way to the plotters. Proceeding from the appraisal which is based on the realities of what has happened, I would like to emphasize the outstanding role of Boris Nikolayevich Yeltsin, the President of Russia, in these events.

Even when I was faced with the ultimatum---to hand over my powers to the Vice-President or resign in order to save the Fatherland, I knew that this venture would fail and that the plotters would suffer a defeat and would have the fate of criminals who are pushing the country and the people to catastrophe in the most difficult time---the time of trials and search for new forms. Nevertheless, thank Goodness that everything ended the way it did, because there had been far reaching designs to deal a blow at the vanguard of democratic forces which are responsible for democratic transformations in the country, despite all complexities. Such was the scheme. The information that the president of Russia had been arrested was part of the blackmail onslaught on the President of the country. By and large, the idea was to deal a strike, to isolate the country's President if he refuses to cooperate with the reactionary forces, and also to isolate the President of the Russian Federation.

The organizers of the plot made their biggest mistake by misjudging our society. We believe that despite all the difficulties our society has become different over the past six years. By uniting, coordinating its efforts and interacting, it can overcome these difficulties and embark on a broad road of continued reforms and transformations, turning into a new society. Thinking that the Union was on the eve of disintegration and that national catastrophes lay in store for it, the putschists hoped that the people would follow them. This was their main miscalculation.

The people did not support the plotters. The Army did not follow them, although attempts were made to draw it into this venture. We have in our possession a growing number of facts which show that the special forces which have been created for combating terrorism were precisely the forces on which the plotters pinned the greatest hopes and which were used, above all, to eliminate the democratic leadership and stop the democratic process.

People refused to do all this. The Armed Forces, including the units which were used (during the putsch) entered into contact with people in the streets and assumed a principled position. This was true of the bulk of the soldiers and officers in these units. The stake on the support of the people and the attempts to play on current hardships failed to help the putschists reach their objective. this was the main cause for their defeat.

We have approached a state in the development of society when everything should undergo change---power, the federation, the economy, property relations and the condition of the people. This will bring us to an altogether different society, in which there will be no room for reactionary forces. In this context, it was a gamble and the last attempt to take revenge and arrest this progressive process."

Answering questions from the audience, Gorbachev broached on the further political course of the country. He emphasized the need for a radical rearrangement of political forces. "We need reliable structures of power and the placement of personnel, which would ensure the continuation of our reforms.

"We have already begun discussing our approaches to many questions. We have decided the question of the country's Defense Minister---former commander-in-chief of the Soviet Air Force Yevgeni Shaposhnikov has been appointed to this post. Vadim Bakatin has been appointed chief of the KGB, and Viktor Barannikov, the Interior Minister of the Russian Federation, has now become the Interior Minister of the USSR. We have also adopted a number of decisions in connection with the forces which should be near the leadership, the President of the country and the President of the Russian Federation who are committed to the policy of continued democratic reform. Proceeding from the lessons of the recent situation, we have created a mechanism whereby if one of the presidents cannot, due to some circumstances, give instructions, his rights and powers are automatically transferred to the other."

Then the President of the USSR pointed to the need to resolve questions connected with the functioning of the Cabinet of Ministers of the USSR. He said that he knew two instances---one fully obvious and the other with some doubts---when members of the Cabinet refused to fulfill the orders of the plotters.

Culture Minister Gubenko refused to collaborate with the plotters and submitted his resignation. I was told that he came out against the plotters at a session of the Cabinet of Ministers, but I have yet to check all this, because I have received some last-minute information that this is not quite so. A more or less critical stand has been assumed by Vladimir Shcherbakov. You think this is not true? Sorry. Boris Nikolayevich gave me short notes of that session when we met, but I had no time to read them. Comrade Primakov told me that Vorontsov expressed a clearly negative position with respect to the decisions of the plotters.

Yeltsin asked Gorbachev to read the notes out loud. He stressed that these notes were taken at the session of the Cabinet at 6 p.m. on August 19th, i.e., at the time the storm of the Russian Parliament was to begin.

Gorbachev: I will read this document in a moment. I will read it with you as I have not yet read it myself. I had differing information about the behavior of the Foreign Minister. He either maneuvered or did not assume a clear position. I have relieved Alexander Bessmertnykh from the duties of the Foreign Minister.

I think that we will be able to find a correct approach. This government as a whole should resign. We are to approach the formation of a new Cabinet of Ministers extremely thoroughly, taking into consideration the competence of every contender, his or her political positions and adherence to democracy and the policy of reforms. We should bear in mind, first and foremost, how the republics are represented. It should be a representative and able Cabinet, because a lot of work needs to be done right away and in the future we should be able to solve problems without delay---people expect us to act like this.

Having exchanged opinions, we have agreed to work out proposals and formulate a common approach in this field. As Alexander Yakovlev said yesterday, we should see to it that there are no more rogues in the Cabinet.

So, the first most important thing is to continue a course of transformation and the formation of a power structure capable of shouldering this responsibility. This will be the best possible guarantee for the future.

We should advance by more rapid strides to the Union Treaty. After all, it was the prospect of signing this treaty, no matter how strongly it might be criticized by different sides, that made the reactionary forces attempt this putsch. These forces know what the new Treaty and its consequences mean.

Of particular importance now is the opinion of all republics. We should keep together at a hard time like this. We can criticize the weak points of the Ogarevo process. There are some weak points, indeed, and we are perfectly aware of them. What is more, it will take strenuous efforts to reach agreement on cooperation.

We are only creating a mechanism which we badly need. That is why all the republics, all their leaders expressed themselves in favor of continued interaction within the framework of an integral Union. Such cooperation is of special importance in the social and economic field in order to solve faster the tasks the crisis has set forth. We are confronted with a very real problem---the problem of survival. Just look what the so-called Emergency Situation Committee played on. It began by proposing precisely what the governments of republics have been doing lately---the elaboration of a food program which is to help us to live up to the next harvest, the problems of heat supply for the coming winter, stabilization of finances in order to clear a way to economic reforms. All these questions are under consideration right now.

We will have to adopt some very unpopular measures. We, all the leaders of the republics, will have to do this. To finish the subject of structures, I think that the Supreme Soviet of the USSR, too, will have to adopt the necessary decisions. The Parliament of the country should act in the wake of what has been manifested in these decisive days. If we had the courage to survive, we will have the courage to bring the putschists to account. By the way, today we agreed with Boris Yeltsin to set up a joint team of investigators from the USSR and the Russian Federation. This decision has been backed by all republics. The team will be supervised by the Procurators-General of the USSR and the Russian Federation. The latter will report to us and we will report to you and the Supreme Soviet of the USSR on the progress of the investigation. We will make the decisions which will be required by the law.

Gorbachev recalled that the Supreme Soviet of the USSR was to hold its session on August 26.

Gorbachev: I think that Russian MPs and Parliamentarians from other republics will take part in its work. The country's Supreme Soviet consists of deputies who, like you, have been elected by the people. I think that it will be up to the mark and adopt the necessary decisions. I am sure that there will be no differences in decision-making. I ask you not to be in a hurry to pass judgements and, in particular, on the Supreme Soviet of the USSR. I know there are people who will have to answer, and they will answer. You, however, should show maturity. The Supreme Soviet of the USSR will begin its work in two days.

Having assumed a firm position in these days of trouble, all the republics supported Russia. By assuming a firm and clear stand, Russia has changed the entire situation and now, after overcoming a crisis, the people of Russia should act jointly with all the Supreme Soviets and peoples of all republics. This is how real Russian people would behave. I will tell you what I think. I hope that you will understand me correctly. A vast opportunity offers itself now for a unifying mission of Russia, the Russian Parliament, the Congress of the Russian Federation's People's Deputies, the Russian Government and the entire Russian people. We, Russians, should fulfill this mission to the end. Do you really think that everything is already behind us? This would be a simplistic view of the situation. The most serious troubles and trials are yet ahead. In the next few months we must do our best for the people to see that things have started changing for the better.

I think that the investigation will help us. We saw these people rear their heads in society, at the plenums of the Communist Party Central Committee and in the Supreme Soviet. We, however, did not yield to them. Nevertheless, they took this step. I think that people in their senses would not do such a thing. These are people who lost their heads, lost a sense of responsibility. It is a clear case of treachery and traitors. I must honestly tell you that for me it is a very hard drama.

This is all the more so as the ultimatum has been delivered by Boldin, my chief of staff, the man whom I completely trusted; Shenin, a member of the Politburo and secretary of the Central Committee; and Baklanov, my deputy in the Defense Council and ex-secretary of the Central Committee. The fourth person who arrived with them was General of the Army Varennikov. He was not a close associate of mine. But later on he went to the Ukraine to give Kravchuk an ultimatum. By the way, we should make a distinction between those who masterminded the whole thing, who joined them later, who wrote telegrams and organized local support committees, on the one hand, and rank-and-file members of the party---workers, collective farmers and intellectuals, on the other, so that to protect the latter. I welcome the position of Anatoli Sobchak, who said that we must not take the strictest measures under law against all those who were involved in the putsch or assisted the putschists by wiping up anti-communist hysteria. This would be used against the people. We all should bear this in mind. I think that we will adopt decisions which are necessary. What is more, I realized it before, for, otherwise, there would not have been the Novo-Ogarevo process, and I have become convinced once again that the lack of unity among the democrats poses the most serious danger. Disunity would be the biggest gift to the hardliners and reactionaries who dream of bringing the country back to the old times. The most important task is to unite the democratic forces. This has been clearly shown by the events of the past few days.

Then the Soviet President read excerpts from the protocol of the closed-door extended meeting of the USSR Cabinet of Ministers held on August 19th under the chairmanship of former Prime Minister Valentin Pavlov. It follows from the text that many officials supported the committee which had been created by political adventurists. It was suggested that each case should be considered separately.

Yeltsin said that after a thorough check-out this information would be published in the daily Izvestia.

Gorbachev: Boris Nikolayevich has sent me a package of decisions which he has made. I have read them. When asked yesterday whether these decisions were legitimate or not, I answered that in the obtaining situation for the country and the Russian leadership there was no other way, in my opinion. All that the Supreme Soviet, the President and the Government of the Russian federation did had been prompted by circumstances and was perfectly legitimate.

Yeltsin: I would ask you to codify this statement by a presidential decree.

Gorbachev: Come on, Boris Nikolayevich, we have not agreed to give away everything right away.

Yeltsin: This is a very serious question.

Gorbachev: When we met today, we had a very serious discussion with Boris Nikolayevich on this question. Yes, all these decrees corresponded to the situation in which they were issued. Therefore, they were quite legitimate because they pursued a definite aim. We agreed that the President of the USSR should issue a corresponding decree to legally codify them. This is a necessary precedent.

Yeltsin: I have put in a special folder all the decrees and resolutions which were adopted in the besieged "White House," I am giving you this folder.

Gorbachev: I am now going to read notes. I have answered some of them. Some authors make their suggestions concerning the KGB and the Armed Forces. By the way, we have relieved Comrade Moiseyev of this duties as the head of the General Staff. Comrade Lobov has taken over. We intend to appoint Comrade Grachev, commander of the land troops, to the post of First Deputy Defense Minister of the USSR.

Yeltsin: Yevgeni Shaposhnikov has been appointed Defense Minister and Grachev, who organized the defense of the "White House," his first deputy and also chairman of the Russian Committee for Defense Questions.

Gorbachev: Indeed, we have adopted many decisions, I will not even mention all of them right now. New proposals will be made in the next day or two. We are in for a clean-up, so to speak. Agreed?

Yeltsin: I have made representations to the President of the country to confer the title of General of the Army on Konstantin Kobets. I have signed a paper on promoting Colonel Rutskoy to the rank of major-General. The President has agreed to such promotions.

Gorbachev: Comrades, I would now like to deal with a couple of tactical questions. Judging by everything, different members of the Emergency Situation Committee bear different responsibility for the coup. As far as I know, Starodubtsev found out that he had been included in the committee only at 10 a.m. on August 19. I am asked whether I have received a letter of explanation from Starodubtsev and what my attitude to it is. I haven't received any letters.

Then questions are asked through the microphones in the hall. The President is reminded that he had once again re-affirmed his allegiance to socialism and intention to improve the Soviet Communist Party. Someone asks whether socialism should be banned from the USSR and the Communist Party disbanded as a criminal organization.

Gorbachev: The question is worded in a very straightforward manner, and I will answer accordingly.

If you take up the problem of banishing socialism from the USSR in the Supreme Soviet and Government of the Russian Federation and even all the Supreme Soviets and Governments, we still won't be able to solve it. It will be a kind of crusade and a latter-day religious war. Socialism is a conviction for some people not only in our country today but also in other countries and in other times. We have declared freedom of convictions and pluralism of opinions. No one has the right to pose the question of driving socialism away. This is a utopia and "witch-hunt." Each determines his or her position, chooses a party or a movement or does not chose any.

Now about the second part of the question. I cannot agree with the proposal to ban the Communist Party as a criminal organization. There are certainly people, trends and groups in this party which do impede the processes of renewal and which have been culprits (in the putsch), for which they should be held responsible either politically or juridically---it depends. But I will never agree that we should disband all communists---workers and peasants. No, it is impermissible to ban the Communist Party as a criminal organization. There are people in its leadership, including Secretariat, who did not have the guts to stand up in defense of their General Secretary and demand a meeting with him. There are party committees which decided to help the so-called Emergency Situation Committee. Each of these people should be held responsible for their actions. But I will never agree to qualify millions of workers and peasants as criminals.

What is more, we have submitted for discussion our new Program. It proclaims ideas and aims which are hard to contest. If this Program is adopted, those who support it will be democrats and they will be with you.

The President is asked about his position on the proposal of a group of Russian Parliamentarians to adopt urgent measures in order to eradicate conditions conducive to coups and other similar situations. In the opinion of these Parliamentarians, these measures should provide for the immediate elimination of parallel administration by party structures. It is suggested that the central bodies of the CPSU and the Russian Communist Party---the Central Committees, the Politburo, regional and territorial party committees, the political bodies inside the KGB, the Interior Ministry, the Army and the Navy---should be disbanded for the transition period, the property of the CPSU and the RCP nationalized and their financial resources, including hard currency, used for social needs. The party property should be nationalized in the atmosphere of openness, under the control of deputies and public commissions; the KGB disbanded, new security bodies created by uniting the corresponding bodies of the republics and frontier troops re-subordinated directly to the President.

Gorbachev: Having made Vadim Bakatin Chairman of the State Security Committee, we have written in the same decree the following: "To submit proposals for the re-organization of this committee." Other questions will be considered in a short while. By the way, the problems which you raise here were discussed during my meeting with the leaders of all the republics. So, we will solve them and elaborate the necessary attitudes and measures without delay. I repeat, however, that everything should be done in a legitimate way.

The President is asked his opinion on the appointment of the key figures in the government, including the Prime Minister. In the opinion of a group of Parliamentarians, this post should be occupied by a representative of Russia. "There is a candidate who has proved to be a very efficient professional---Ivan Silayev, if he agrees, of course."

Gorbachev: Boris Nikolayevich knows my position. I think that the President of the country and the Prime Minister should represent Russia, the vice-president another republic, preferably a Central Asian one.

I have not given up this position. As for the other part of the question, we have discussed the situation around the Council of Ministers, which is very acute, indeed. We agreed to think it over during the next few days and work out a common approach. It is important to form a coalition government with the participation of all the republics.

One of the MPs says: anti-communism is a response to communism and a return to the norm in the same way as anti-fascism is a response to fascism and a return to the norm. There is either a fascist or a communist hysteria. That is why the CPSU, which from the outset was created on criminal principles, is a party of betrayal. What prevents the President from issuing a decree on sealing all the buildings which belong to the CPSU? According to this MP, the Central Committee is transferring huge sums of money, including in hard currency, from its bank accounts. This should be stopped.

All these questions are to be settled in the next few days, replies the President. "That is why I will not dwell on this issue now. If anything illegal is really taking place, I agree that measures need to be taken to stop it."

Yeltsin: We have taken such measures and sealed the Central Committee building.

Gorbachev: Try to control your emotions. We badly need clear heads on our shoulders now.

Then the President talks about allegations that he knew about plans for the putsch. Some people who claim this refer to the interview which Anatoli Lukyanov gave on August 19.

Gorbachev: The forces which have suffered a defeat are capable of any concoctions. This is a gross lie and a rude attempt to cast a shade on the President and his reputation. They failed to blackmail me into signing any kind of document or making a statement. I then knew that they would do their utmost to get me into a condition which would accord with their statement on my alleged disability to fulfil my constitutional functions. I have not seen or read (Lukyanov's) statement. If he says so, he is simply a crook.

Gorbachev is reminded that during the Fourth Congress Russia's Vice-President Rutskoy waited in the President's office for three hours but the President did not receive him. The events of the past few days have shown, an MP says, that the Russian Parliament is your only reliable support. Have you realized this?

Gorbachev: I think we need each other as people committed to the idea of democratic transformation. A rift or a split between us would be tantamount to the end of this process.

The President is told that in his statements he describes mostly the way he was treated in his Crimea residence, including the behavior of his granddaughter. Today, too, some MPs say, we have heard practically nothing about what you are going to do further with the exception of a few personnel changes. We haven't heard anything about the Russian property.

Gorbachev: I have said that we have come up right to the implementation of specific measures designed to bring about renewal---the signing of a Union Treaty, the implementation of the anti-crisis program, food and fuel problems and the stabilization of finances. To do all these necessary things, we need to re-group our forces and create new legislative and executive authorities capable of assuming responsibility, commanding the trust of the people and ready to finish what we have started.

We have come up to a stage at which specific tasks of democratic transformation should be carried through.

Yeltsin: Just a moment, Mikhail Sergeyevich. The question was about property ownership. I want to remind you that even prior to these events we agreed that if you do not make up your mind about the transfer to Russia of all property in its territory, then the President of Russia would issue a corresponding decree. On August 20th I signed a decree in accordance with which all the property in the territory of the Russian Federation, with the exception of the functions delegated to the Union, belongs to Russia. You have said today that you will sign a decree confirming all the decrees I have issued over this period.

Gorbachev: I do not think that you have forced me into a trap. The wording should be more precise.

Yeltsin said that he had signed a decree suspending activities of the Russian Communist Party, pending the investigation of its participation in the coup. "This is perfectly legitimate. The Russian Communist Party has not been registered by the Justice Ministry of the Russian Federation," he says.

Gorbachev: Be democrats to the end, and then all the genuine democrats and sober-minded people will be on your side.

The President is asked his opinion about the people who headed the state committees. Is the President capable of qualifying the position of the secretaries of party committees up to the Central Committee? What will the President's next steps be?

Gorbachev: If there is a need for the most decisive measures justified by the situation, I will take such measures. I am ready for this morally and politically. We should show that we can solve things in a legitimate and democratic manner. I will insist on precisely such a way of action. But this should not be to the detriment of our resolve and firmness.

Yeltsin: I can confirm that during our today's one-on-one conversation which lasted for an hour and a half Mikhail Sergeyevich firmly assured me that corresponding measures would be taken with respect to the persons who were involved in the coup, whether directly or indirectly. These should be resolute and stern measures prompted by the law. There should be no mercy on these people.

Several more questions are asked from the audience. Certain things were explained and clarified.

At the request of the deputies, the President laid down his attitude to Alexander Yakovlev and Eduard Sheverdnadze. "They have been with me since April 1985, sharing a hard search for the right way and also the mistakes that have been made. I most of all appreciate their contribution to the choice of a way and the elaboration of a course.

A voice from the audience: But they have resigned.

Gorbachev: I am against the resignation of both of them. But I cannot keep persuading them if they wish it their own way.

(TASS)

STATEMENT BY MIKHAIL GORBACHEV ON AUGUST 24, 1991

The Secretariat and Politburo of the CC CPSU did not speak out against the coup d'etat. The Central Committee failed to take a determined stand of condemnation and resistance, did not stir the communists to action against the breach of constitutional legality. Among the plotters were members of the party leadership, and some party committees and mass media of information backed up the actions of the state criminals. This placed millions of communists in a false position.

Many party members refused to collaborate with the plotters, denounced the coup and joined in the struggle against it. Nobody has any moral right to accuse all the communists indiscriminately, and I as President consider myself duty-bound to protect them as citizens from unjustified charges.

In these circumstances the CPSU Central Committee should take a difficult, but honest decision on self-dissolution. The future of republican communist parties and local party organizations will be decided by themselves.

I do not consider for myself possible the further performance of my functions as General Secretary of the CC CPSU and relinquish the appropriate powers. I believe that democratic-minded communists who preserved loyalty to constitutional legality and the course for the renovation of society will come out for the formation on a new basis of a party able together with all progressive forces to become actively involved in the continuation of sweeping democratic changes in the interests of the working people.

Krasnaya Zvezda, August 27, 1991

M. Gorbachev
August 24, 1991

SUICIDES AND BONNER COMMENTS

Marshall Sergei Akhromeyev Commits Suicide Two Days After Soviet Putsch Fails

Marshal Sergei Akhromeyev, 68, Chief of the General Staff of the USSR Armed Forces before 1988 and since recently a personal military aide to USSR President Mikhail Gorbachev hanged himself in his Kremlin office at about 10 a.m. on August 24. It was not until 10 p.m. that his body was found.

It is anybody's guess why the Marshall decided to take his life. So far the press has carried no information on his direct involvement in the attempted coup d'etat. Recently the USSR Procurator-General has announced that the plotters mentioned Akhromeyev as a participant in their preliminary testimony. But the final judgement will be passed only after the results of an inquiry are made public.

Akhromeyev left several notes for his family and friends before he hanged himself. Their content hasn't been disclosed yet. He said in one of them that "everything that I have dedicated my life to is falling apart."

Moscow News, No. 36, 1991

Yelena Bonner
Widow of Andrei Sakharov

I'll say a good thing about Gorbachev. It is under him that a new generation of people has grown up who will never agree to live under communism. They just won't agree, this is it. No matter how this communism is referred to, autocracy, Orthodoxy, a Renewed Union of Sovereign Republics, or any other names. People have opened their eyes, have learned to tell truth from lies (Andrei Sakharov is a perfect example) will live in genuinely sovereign states. I hope that such states will be friendly towards one another if their leaders don't give way to the euphoria of the victory.

My eyes opened a long time ago, but I'm grateful to Gorbachev for opening the eyes of millions of my fellow countrymen. On a human level I am happy that the mafia he hand-picked himself didn't finish off himself or his family. I have lived a long and happy life as a woman I can see very well the love he and Raisa Maximovna share. I like it when there is love. It doesn't happen often. I can see it in Boris Yeltsin. It doesn't mean though that I will keep silence if Yeltsin gets carried away by his ideas of great Russia and a great power. Whom will such power be used against? Against the people who only yesterday shielded the White House with their bodies and against other nations as well.

CPSU CC Business Manager Nikolai Krunchina Kills Himself Five Days After the Putsch

Business Manager of the CPSU CC Nikolai Kruchina threw himself off the balcony in his apartment on the night of August 25th. His wife and younger son were at home and they would have woken up if there had been any struggle or shouting. There is a number of other reasons that allow the prosecutor's office of the Leninsky district of Moscow to argue that it is a case of suicide.

Kruchina left two notes. One was found on a coffee table in the apartment's hallway immediately, the other was found on the body. The message was tragic and boiled down to this: "...I am not a traitor or a plotter... I am a coward." Kruchina wrote that he wasn't guilty and asked this to be told to the people. He wrote that his "only fault was that I signed an instruction for the protection of these secretaries" (he must have referred to the members of the State Committee for the State of Emergency."

His apartment was searched by three investigators for extraordinary cases. No traces were found of any destroyed documents. The investigating officers confiscated certain documents. The titles and the signatures under them indicated that they were of extreme importance.

As Putsch Falls Through USSR Interior Minister Boris Pugo Commits Suicide

Boris Pugo was a very strong-willed and reserved person. Everybody thought that arresting him would be a problem. He wasn't to be found anywhere at first. The arresting party came to the Ministry, made a lot of phone calls. He was nowhere to be found. The government phones were silent. It was between 7 a.m. through 9 a.m. All of a sudden the Chairman of the Russian KGB got through to Pugo at his home phone. Pugo picked up the receiver. The caller introduced himself. After a long pause Pugo said, "Well, come here, we'll have a talk." Within a few minutes three cars pulled to his house in Ryleev Street. Officers climbed the stairs, began to ring the door bell. At last an elderly person slowly opened the door. He was asked if something bad had happened. He answered in the positive. Pugo was lying on the floor in a room. He had shot himself in the mouth. Next to him was his wife. She was in a terrible state but her condition was better. Blood was all over her. Reportedly there were three cartridge-cases on the floor.

Rossiiskaya Gazeta 3, Tuesday, August 27

DECREES BY THE PRESIDENT OF THE USSR ON THE PROPERTY OF THE COMMUNIST PARTY OF THE SOVIET UNION

1. Soviets of People's Deputies shall assume the custody of the property of the CPSU. The questions of its further appropriation shall be resolved strictly in accordance with the laws of the USSR and the republics on property and public associations.
2. Pursuant to existing legislation, Soviets of People's Deputies shall take measures for providing jobs and social security for the staff of the party committees which cease their activities. law enforcement and other state agencies shall prevent any violation of civil rights.

President of the Union of Soviet Socialist Republics
M. Gorbachev
The Kremlin, Moscow,
August 24, 1991

On Terminating the Activity of Political Parties and Political Movements in the Armed Forces of the USSR, Law Enforcement Agencies and the State Apparatus

1. The Activity of political parties and political movements in the Armed Forces of the USSR, USSR Ministry of the Interior, State Security Committee, other law-enforcement agencies, railway troops and all other military formations and bodies of the state apparatus shall be terminated.
2. Members of political parties and political movements engaged in the above mentioned structures and bodies shall exercise their constitutional right to participate in political activity outside such bodies during non-working hours.

President of the Union of Soviet Socialist Republics
M. Gorbachev
The Kremlin, Moscow
August 24, 1991

UNITED NEWSPAPER
(OBSHCHAYA GAZETA)

Registered by special decision of Russia's Ministry for the Press and Information (registration number 1054) on August 20, 1991

Titles of contributing periodicals (left):

ARGUMENTY I FAKTY
COMMERSANT
KOMSOMOLSKAYA PRAVDA
KURANTY
MEGAPOLIS EXPRESS
MOSCOW NEWS
MOSCKOVSKY KOMSOMOLETS
NEZAVISIMAYA GAZETA (Independent Newspaper)
ROSSIYSKAYA GAZETA (Russia's Newspaper)
ROSSIYSKIYE VESTI
STOLITSA

DEAR READERS AND FRIENDS!

The United Newspaper came out during the August putsch as a joint effort of many periodicals. Xeroxed and duplicated in Moscow and Leningrad, it was circulated in certain areas where crowds of people gathered to share objective information on the events.

Today when the constitutional order is restored, our periodicals, back on their routine work, will come out in time. We want, however, to produce a further *United Newspaper* issue, printed under normal conditions and complete with reports on the last night of the putsch and its collapse.

DEMOCRACY SHOULD LEARN TO DEFEND ITSELF

Statement by the Editors-in-Chief of the Periodicals Banded in Violation of the Law on the Press.

Our *United Newspaper* is the result of our common plight: the country is struck down by an anticonstitutional coup. The plotters who betrayed the supreme power bodies started their rule by prohibiting Soviet and Moscow democratic periodicals, which countered their views. The ban on free information---the greatest achievement of perestroika---explains one of the putschists' aims. They inevitably wanted to restore the punitive regime, make the most of their last opportunity and stake everything on one last go. There reprisals of the press today are bound to be transformed into a nation-wide purge tomorrow.

How can one preserve freedom and consequently human dignity in such conditions? By following the Law and those democratic principles which have become part and parcel of our life. We are loyal to the Law on the Press, an immovable tenet for us. The putschists prevented us from publishing our newspapers normally and we consequently launched the *United Newspaper*, to be compiled jointly by varying staff and to come out every day as of August 20.

We abide by the Law. Reader and citizen! Follow the Law---that will be your conscious non-obedience to the plotters' decrees, conductive to the failure of their venture.

Time calls for unity. And this cohesion of all the democratic forces is gaining momentum and frustrating the coup. This is the aim, which has united us, representatives of newspapers of diverse trends, who share the opinion that democracy should defend itself.

Vladimir VOLIN (Megapolis-Express),
Pavel GUSEV (Moskovsky Komsomolets),
Valeri KUCHER (Rossiyskiye Vesti),
Valentin LOGUNOV (Rossiyskaya Gazeta),
Andrei MALGIN (Stolitsa),
Anatoli PANKOV (Kuranty),
Vladislav STARKOV (Argumenty I Fakty),
Vitali TRETYAKOV (Nezavisimaya Gazeta),
Vladislav FRONIN (Komsomolskaya Pravda),
Valdimir YAKOVLEV (Commersant),
Yegor YAKOVLEV (Moscow News).

THE COUP: COMPETITION OF POSSIBLE SCENARIOS

By Alexander Surmava

The coup attempt that luckily failed has inspired political leaders and journalists to write numerous commentaries, in which they not only describe well-known facts but also put forward quite improbable versions of the events.

Analyzing the attempted coup, commentators explain in different ways why the coup leaders, who had the biggest army and police in the world, were so inefficient.

All existing versions of the coup give two diametrically opposite explanations for its motives: some say that the coup was a genuine attempt by the conservative forces to retain power; other claim it was a provocation staged by democrats to get rid of their political opponents. The advocates of the first theory have no doubt that the coup was organized by communist party apparatchiks, who feared losing power, the world's largest army of generals and, finally, the defense industry tycoons, who are watching with horror the dwindling supply of petrodollars. The names and positions of the members of the Emergency Committee bear this theory out well.

However, the public wonders whether Gorbachev himself was behind the coup attempt and experts differ on this matter, explaining Gorbachev's behavior in different ways.

Though most allegations on this theme do not credit Gorbachev with being the leader of the coup, the role accorded to him in the events of August 19--22 is an extremely sinister and treacherous one. According to this version, he not only initiated the putsch, but cleverly organized everything so that any outcome would guarantee him political advantage. In this case, Anatoly Lukyanov is not a man who betrayed the ideals he shared with Gorbachev when they were university students, but a secret ally and agent of Gorbachev in the camp of the coup organizers.

Like any other, this version has its opponents. The latter say if Gorbachev had supported the coup leaders, he would have risked too much, if not everything, no matter whether the coup succeeded or not. In any case,

Gorbachev would have lost much of his power because any of the possible outcomes would lead to absolute domination of one political force, which he would not be able to lead owing to his character: Gorbachev has long been known as a master of maneuver and compromise.

This version of the coup has more intricate modifications. According to one of them, the organizers of the Satanic coup were both the president of the Soviet Union and president of Russia, who wanted to defeat with one blow the opposition to democratic reforms in the communist party and in military circles. Those who dispute this theory say that it was senseless for the two legally elected presidents, who had all the powers inherent in their position, and who had formed a secret alliance to get rid of their political opponents in such an extravagant and risky manner.

Lastly, the most paradoxical version, which appeals to its authors by the bold paradox it is built on, is that the coup was organized by Yeltsin who wanted to remove his enemies by that treacherous method and successfully carried out his plan. This version has a purely ethical lapse: it makes the defeated leaders of the coup appear too helpless and foolish.

The second question that gives no rest to all the participants in the defense of the Russian parliament building is why the coup leaders were so indecisive, why the did not arrest the Russian president and his team in the early hours of the coup, why the did not cut off all communications with the outside world and why they allowed Yeltsin to lead the insurgents angered by the coup. It is unbelievable that the people who thoroughly studied Lenin's writings on this subject and had a unique experience in organizing "popular revolutions" in Africa, Afghanistan and other countries lacked the required experience.

There are two possible answers to this question. The first and most paradoxical one is that there was no coup and that someone, mostly likely Gorbachev, just played a clever game. He might have done that of his own free will or under the force of circumstances. If the latter is true, it is a detective and psychological rather than political version.

Other experts believe that all the "odd" circumstances of the coup can be easily explained by strictly political reasons. There are, in principle, two possible scenarios of a coup d'etat. One is the hard or "Chilean" version with all its well-known concomitants mentioned above: mass arrests of opposition politicians, the seizure of the telephone exchange, the telegraph, etc. The other is "soft" when the head of state is removed in a more or less "legal" way and all the other are terrorized into submission without bloodshed.

To stage a coup of the first kind its organizers should have a leader capable of organizing mass murders to intimidate the public. Secondly, the coup leaders should have enough ruthless troops to eliminate all their opponents and do so not only fast but with sinister panache that would make blood chill in the veins of two or three generations of spectators. Finally, the coup leaders should feel confident enough in the economic sense to ignore international public opinion and possible economic and political sanctions.

Our coup leaders had no Fuehrer or father of the nation. The troops, which are formed on the national-political principle, did not justify their expectations either. The officers' corps of the Soviet Army has always been formed mainly from Slavs for safety's sake. One could count on such troops in non-Slav regions, but it is a great risk to use them in Moscow or Sverdlovsk. Lastly, it is absurd to stage a blood-bath a hundred yards away from the American Embassy and continue to beg grain and credits from the Americans. The best friend of our coup leaders, Saddam Hussein, has had the opportunity to realize this lately.

So, the Gang of Eight could only use the "soft" version and they failed nevertheless because it is no longer possible to suppress this country in upheaval without first drowning its people in blood.

But then again, this is just one of the possible versions.

Kommersant No. 24 (84),
August 19–26, 1991

GROUP ALPHA DID NOT STRIKE—WHEN PEOPLE DEFENDING RUSSIA'S WHITE HOUSE WERE PREPARED TO FIGHT TO THE END

By Andrei Abrosimov and Andrei Zhdankin

For three days and nights during the foiled coup d'etat in August, crowds guarding the Russian parliament building were ready to stand siege. *Rossiyskaya Gazeta* (Russian Gazette) reporters were among the defenders of Russia's "White House." They can confirm that the biggest threat was posed by the KGB's Alpha Group. Contradictory and fearsome rumors about it kept circulating for three days and nights. To this day, the public knows little about the group. Meanwhile, it is a crack task force capable of putting up a deadly fight and attaining virtually any mission. Had it been put into action, the fate of the "White House" and, possibly, of democracy in our country could have been different. But Group Alpha did not strike.

Some time ago reporters from the *Rossiyskaya Gazeta* had a meeting with two of the group's commanding officers at the headquarters of the Russian KGB. We were seated face to face and could ask virtually any questions. This is evidently one of the consequences of the victory for democracy. In the words of Alpha's press officer Nikolai Maklakov, who took part in the meeting, it was the first time in secret service history that active members of such a group granted an interview to media representatives. They declined to be photographed even from the back, though.

We talked with Mikhail Golovatov, whom the Soviet president appointed commander of the group a few days ago, and his deputy Sergei Goncharov.

Question: Whom is Group Alpha subordinated to?
Answer: In accordance with the presidential order, the group is subordinated personally to the President of the USSR and, in the event of his inability to issue commands, to the President of the RSFSR. The order was issued a few days ago. We were summoned to see Bakatin, the new KGB chief, who told us twice in his office that from that time on our group was

taking orders only from the USSR President. Before that we had been subordinated to the KGB chief and organizationally belonged to the KGB's Seventh Directorate.

Question: What orders did you receive from the State of Emergency Committee starting from August 19th and during the putsch?

Answer: The group was put on alert. The group commander arrived at the base at about 5:30 p.m. August 19th. He assembled the officers and ordered preparatory measures for an operation to gain control of the Russian parliament building. The first question was who had issued such an order, because the commander---and we perfectly knew it---was only communicating it to us. We were told twice, clearly and in no uncertain terms, that the order had come from the government. We asked what government had ordered the assault. The answer was the same: "it's a government order. The assault shall take place at 3 a.m. August 20."

Question: What do preparatory measures usually include:

Answer: To use the military language, we had to know the alignment of forces, the situation in which we and the opposite side would find themselves.

We knew that the building's defenders were armed. Boris Nikolayevich (Yeltsin) was guarded by his security detail. These were people whom, to a certain extent, we knew personally. That had a certain impact on the entire situation. According to our information, there were about 500 armed men in the building. A heavy truck full of small arms arrived at the building. Hand grenades and, possibly, grenade launchers were distributed. People were getting ready to defend mother Russian and their president to the end. We knew where Yeltsin and other leaders were, we also knew the location of offices on the stories of the building.

Our mission was as follows: the entire Group Alpha, fully armed and equipped for the occasion, was to storm the "White House," make its way into the building and take it under control.

We knew that six tanks and fifteen armored personnel carriers were stationed near the building. If the tanks had opened fire at us, many members of the group would have died, but the rest would have attained the mission anyway.

Question: What weapons did the group carry?

Answer: All we can tell you is what weapons the group should usually carry while pursuing missions of that kind.

Question: Did you have any special equipment, additional weapons, such as grenade launchers and so forth?

Answer: Yes, we had all of these. We can tell you about small arms. We are not trying to conceal that we have a special kind of arms but their possible uses are, if you excuse us, a secret. The "White House" could not have possibly held out against a group armed with such systems.

Question: Did your group, as rumors have it, carry a list of twelve persons who were to be arrested?

Answer: Our task was to storm the building and take it under control. The group can fulfill commands while its individual members are scattered throughout a building or are in different buildings. Each of us carries a portable radio and can act autonomously. We did not have such a list. It was not communicated to us. Our mission was the storming of the building, that is, the beginning of special combat operations.

That would have caused bloodshed, not ordinary bloodshed, mind you, but a sea of blood. We had information that the defenders were determined to stand to the last man, but they could not have withstood the onslaught of professionals like ourselves. To put it straight, we would have attained our mission in twenty, O.K. let's say, twenty-five minutes. But there would have been many casualties.

Question: Were any other tasks entrusted to Group Alpha during the coup?

Answer: No, the only task was to storm the building and take it under control. That was, the way we see it, the main task of the putsch in general.

Question: Did the decision to ignore the order come to men and officers simultaneously? Were there any differences on that score?

Answer: We cannot say that such a decision came to use at once. We were literally startled when we heard the order. Back then we sat shoulder to shoulder the way we are sitting now. I pushed him with my elbow and said: "I won't go." And he answered: "Neither will I." So we made the same decision. The commanding officer left the base and we assembled the officers and told them the following:

"Let's hear everyone of you. And let everyone of you tell the rest about the decision he made." They rose to their feet one after another and said that the order was illegal and unconstitutional and that they won't fulfill it. After that we asked squad commanders to assemble their personnel, communicate the order to every man and ask everyone to say what they thought of it.

Twenty minutes later the officers returned and said their men would not fulfill such an order. They said they won't go. "And we won't lead you there," we told them.

Although we were confident that our men would not let us down, we felt enormous relief. Otherwise, it would have appeared that two senior commanders of the group mutinied. You can imagine what such a situation would have meant. Don't forget that we are servicemen.

It should be stressed that everyone faced a very difficult choice. We are servicemen and we dared question the order. No such thing had happened in the group and it was founded back in 1974. Nothing of that kind could even be imagined.

Question: Did you figure out what would be in store for you if the coup succeeded?
Answer: Yes, we did. If the coup succeeds, we reckoned, the best thing will be dismissal without pension. The unit will be disbanded and, you know, to be fired is a terrible thing for people who served with the group for many years. We also thought of the worst outcome.
Question: Was pressure put to bear on you to make you fulfill the order?
Answer: And fairly strong pressure, too. While we sat in our office we had to answer numerous calls from officers higher up the line. The group commander would come and go, come and go. He was summoned to see senior officials.
Question: For brainwashing?
Answer: Yes. After returning from each such visit he put pressure on us so that we begin the operation.

Weapons and ammunition had already been distributed among our men. All we had to do was board our vehicles and take up initial positions for the assault.
Question: Can you name your former commander?
Answer: Major-General Viktor Karpukhin, Hero of the Soviet Union.
Question: If we understood you correctly he was ready to fulfill the order.
Answer: Without questioning it.
Question: If the group had stormed the building after all would there have been casualties?
Answer: Try to figure it out yourself. Some 10,000 people were defending the parliament. At the beginning of the assault the crowd would have rushed back from the building and then---such things usually happen in situations like that---it would have moved closer again. It's hard to imagine the number of casualties.
Question: Let's approach the matter from a different standpoint. What did your group save the defenders from?
Answer: Our group saved the country from a civil war. With the end of the assault a civil war would have broken out in the country: a certain part of the armed forces supported the State of Emergency Committee, while the other backed Russia and democracy.
Question: When did you realize that the putsch was a flop?
Answer: When squad commanders told us that personnel would not storm the building and when we announced that we would not lead them into the assault. Our boys went back to their rooms to rest and we kept waiting for Karpukhin. We were absolutely calm, for we knew that the war would not begin.
Question: Did anyone from your group decide to resign after all that?
Answer: On the contrary. We are now barraged with calls. To say that people thank us would be an understatement. It does not adequately describe

what our callers tell us. These are former members of Group Alpha who resigned earlier because of age or for reasons of health, ordinary KGB officers and those senior KGB officials who did not support the State of Emergency Committee. it should be noted that a major, if not actually a larger, part of KGB officers were on our side and did not support the conspirators.

We would like to stress that it is wrong to consider the KGB to be a silent, thoughtless and obedient force which can become an instrument in the hands of the KGB chiefs. Six years of perestroika have had a tremendous impact on us too.

Question: How many officers and men does the group comprise?

Answer: You see, there are questions which we cannot answer. (Lieutenant-General Rasshchepov said yesterday that the group consisted of about 200 men and had a total of about 500 men together with regional units.)

Question: What is the average age of the group's members?

Answer: We, for example, belong to the elder generation. (Both men are in their early forties---Interviewers.) There are people who joined the group five and ten years ago. The average age is 30--32. Not so long ago the group received a reinforcement consisting of young men who haven't taken part in a single operation. For them the planned operation would have been the first and, honestly speaking, probably the last one.

Question: How much did the members of Group Alpha get?

Answer: We almost do not differ from other divisions of the KGB. The only thing is that about a month ago a 20 percent bonus was introduced. Medium-level personnel get paid 420 roubles a month plus that bonus, plus the pay for the officer's rank. This works out to about 550--600 roubles a month which is peanuts in present-day conditions. No one gets more than 700 roubles with the exception of commanders. And, of course, there are benefits for which all servicemen qualify. In our case it is a special estimation of the length of service in view of the special conditions in which we operate.

Question: General Karbainov, the KGB public relations chief, confirmed that Group Alpha was in Vilnius, capital of Lithuania, during the January events there. Could you tell us about its role in more detail?

Answer: Once the fact was admitted, it would be stupid to mislead the public and deny that we were there. It's better to tell the truth, no matter how bitter it may be.

Yes, we were in Vilnius at that time and our mission took us to the TV center on the night of January 12--13. The group was airlifted to the Lithuanian capital by special flights. We were based at Northern Army Base there. In the evening we were ordered to make our way into the TV center---it was surrounded by the public---take it under control and guard all transmitting systems and equipment until the arrival of new television engineers and technicians.

We carried weapons that are usually issued during such operations: AK-74U submachine guns with blank cartridges (one magazine per every member of the group) and special attachments which are used when blank cartridges are fired, PM pistols with sixteen live cartridges (two eight-cartridge clips), walkie-talkies, protective helmets, flak jackets, flashlights and knives.

We want to tell you with all responsibility that we did not fire a single shot---let us emphasize---not a single shot.

Terrible things are said about us now: it is alleged that Group Alpha can accomplish any mission and will stop at nothing. This is not so. In actual fact we carried out operations for public good: we freed children and passengers taken hostage inside airliners, we stopped and got criminals with explosive devices in very dangerous situations.

During the putsch, according to our information, the defenders of the "White House" were told they would die as soon as Group Alpha arrived.

We want to tell the public that it is not so. Group Alpha has proved that it includes intelligent human beings who can see what is right and what is wrong and, most importantly, who care for the country and Russia in particular, just as all ordinary people. We are the same human beings with our own problems: we realized only too well what we were ordered to do. This is why we ignored that criminal order.

STATE SECURITY WHICH IS DANGEROUS TO THE STATE

By Vadim Bakatin about KGB

Vadim Bakatin was born in 1937. Since 1973 he had been doing party work as Secretary of the Kemerovo Regional Committee of the CPSU, inspector of the CPSU Central Committee and First Secretary of the Kirov and Kemerovo Regional Committees of the CPSU. He was Soviet Minister of the Interior. Under strange circumstances he was replaced by Boris Pugo. After the failure of the coup he was appointed new head of the KGB.

Question: How did your family take your new appointment?
Answer: My family? I haven't seen my children for four days, only my wife. She cries and asks me what is to become of us. I'm trying to console her. She says that our son can't get his discharge---he has 29 clearance chits to sign yet. You see, I had one son working at the KGB.
Question: Why is he getting his discharge?
Answer: He was dismissed.
Question: By whom?
Answer: By me.
Question: Why? What did he do?
Answer: Nothing.
Question: ?!
Answer: But this is only natural. I think that I must not have any family relations with my subordinates.
Question: O.K., that's clear now. What did you feel when you moved to Lubyanka? A shock, a surprise or a disappointment? What impressed you most? Did you ever picture yourself as head of the KGB?
Answer: Frankly speaking, I did, but I never thought about it seriously. My friends called me to tell that it was rumored that I would be appointed for sure, but I didn't think about it seriously.

As for shocks and surprises, there were none, even when I more or less acquainted myself with the KGB structure. If all unnecessary departments are abolished, KGB will be smaller in size than, say, the Ministry of the Interior.

You see, the worst thing is that the KGB as it was had the monopoly on government communication, total shadowing, secrecy, coding and decoding of documents, protection of the Soviet borders and even the President. I am sure that it played a decisive role in the coup. It's the structure of the security bodies which presented a danger to the USSR---that's the paradox. My task is to turn the KGB into an organization really ensuring the country's security rather than studying public moods and protecting the higher echelons of power from them.

Let everybody do their duty. The government should protect itself, law enforcement bodies should watch over the interests of the individual and property, and we should engage only in intelligence, counterintelligence and, if you like, crimes committed by high-ranking Soviet Government officials. The rest does not concern us.

Question: They say that Gorbachev offered to give you a promotion. Is it true?

Answer: Yes, it is. But I refused. What for? I think that in future this post will be held by a civilian.

Question: Are you a general?

Answer: I'm Lieutenant-General.

Question: Do you ever wear your uniform?

Answer: I think I wore it three times. No, two. I put it on for the first time on Militia Day in 1988. I didn't know then whether I should wear it all the time or on special occasions. For the second time I put it on in 1989, also on Militia Day. I don't think that I will ever wear it again.

Question: Do you have bodyguards?

Answer: This is a good question. No, I don't have bodyguards yet. I've never had any, even when I worked at the Security Council, although according to my position I could have a bodyguard. Plekhanov, head of the KGB bodyguard department, who is under arrest now, told me that they had to guard me. I signed a paper saying that I didn't need a bodyguard.

But now...Bodyguards are a serious matter, a political matter if you like. Now I'm heading a department which will deal with serious and even dangerous problems. So I don't know yet. I've got to think about it. But I don't have my own bodyguards yet.

Question: I understand that you don't have them in the figurative sense of the word either. The Government Protection Board has been transferred to the government, hasn't it?

Answer: Yes, it has, and the KGB still has to get rid of many things. Let's analyze its different structures. Do we need intelligence? Yes, we do. Should it be made into a separate organization? If you mention it in your article, write four "no's". I'm not sure. I have to think about it. Let's just say that it is necessary.

What about counterintelligence? No doubt, it is the duty of the KGB. Military intelligence? Let the military do it. Then come frontier troops. Should we guard the border? Yes, we should, but it isn't KGB's business. Government communication? It will be maintained by a separate department. Perhaps, it will lease the government dials to businessmen for big money--- it's O.K. with me. Coding, decoding, special troops, protection of the constitutional system, inspectors' control and so on. We should think seriously about that. Of course, we may use some of it but not of this size and in this form. For example, I think we need the operations and technical department but it should perform the tasks of the new KGB which I already described. As for the protection and maintenance of government dachas, let the government take care of it. Do we need an investigating department? Yes, we do. An analytical department? Naturally. Any serious organization must clearly see its prospects. A military construction board? It mostly engaged in the construction of frontier installations and houses for the staff. We still need it. What else? The personnel department. We need it but its staff should be reduced. Naturally, we need the secretariat and the financial department. The expediency of the KGB's higher school will be discussed. The archives should be transferred...

Question: I wanted to talk about it in more detail. You must have been asked to publish the lists of secret agents, haven't you?

Answer: Yes, I have. I want to say outright that I won't publish these lists in any case. That would have meant splitting up society. No, never. Just think about it. For example, the KGB tried to "recruit" my wife when a student. She refused to cooperate but her card is still in the archives. There are thousands of examples like this. Many people agree to be KGB agents, but not for the fun of it. We should adopt a normal law on the operations and investigation activity to recruit the agents not on the basis of by-laws written nobody knows when but in a civilized way. No doubt we need a network of agents. There is one in all civilized countries.

Question: What do you think about KGB agents who use civilian professions as a cover?

Answer: Let's get it straight. There are intelligence officers who really have a legal and an illegal profession. I beg your pardon, how else can they do intelligence work? The so-called "officers of the active reserve" who were implanted in different organizations with the only purpose of spying on their employees is quite a different matter. I'm against this structure. I ordered to give me the lists of these people to recall them.

Question: I wanted to ask you about eavesdropping. Do you know anything about it and are you going to do anything about it?

Answer: No, I don't know anything yet, I didn't have time to learn. But I think I'll find it out. So far I have dismissed the head of the 12th department who, as I understand, has something to do with it. I appointed a woman general to this post and told her to curtail such work. Under the law, eavesdropping is allowed only with the sanction of the public prosecutor if proceedings have been instituted against the person and it may help the investigation. The charges must be serious enough.

Question: What will become of the "Alpha" unit which is now subordinate to the president?

Answer: I think for the time being it will remain so. But if this group, which consists of serious officers, is given to us, I won't refuse. These boys will be useful to us.

Question: I was told that the atmosphere in the KGB was tense, to put it mildly. A new broom, you know.

Answer: I want to make it clear that there will never be any repressions, persecution and unwarranted dismissals on ideological grounds.

Question: When and how do you get a rest? I heard that you draw in your free time, but now you have no time for landscapes, do you?

Answer: Yes, I do. Recently I had a good rest. After the election of the President of Russia I had 40 days to myself. Besides, I feel ill and got a sick leave. In a word, I had time to write a small book on my experience as Minister of the Interior and why I left this post.

Then I hired a team of builders and we built a house according to my own design. It was such fun! I sawed, carried things and dug the earth to my heart's content. Of course, there is still a lot to do. I didn't have much time for drawing this time—I made only two sketches.

Question: What house did you build?

Answer: A country-house, of course. I joined the neighborhood association of country-house owners.

I REJOINED AN ENTIRELY DIFFERENT ORGANIZATION

Colonel Vladimir Rubanov, the author of a series of theoretical works on national security problems, has been appointed head of the KGB's analytical department. Before that, he had worked for the Russian Republic's Innovation Fund, although he is not a novice in the KGB. He joined the organization in Voronezh back in 1971 after graduating from the local polytechnical school. Starting in 1982, he worked for the KGB's Second Directorate and later became head of a division at the Institute of Information Research (a research establishment of the KGB), where he became one of the architects of the state-sponsored program for reforming the system of state secrecy. No sooner had he and his colleagues come up with more or less radical suggestions (by the standards of that time, that is) than the program was canceled and Rubanov was forced to resign. In 1989--90 he worked as an assistant to Vadim Bakatin, at that time USSR Minister of the Interior, and then for a short while served as Deputy Chairman of the Russian Republic's State Committee for Public Security.

Question: You rejoined the KGB after a certain interval. Have you noticed any changes?

Answer: To say there have been changes would be an understatement. I rejoined an entirely different organization. Reform is in full swing at the KGB. No one's waiting for any theoretical plans or coordination programs.

Question: What are the changes?

Answer: On a very general plane, things that were quite obvious to the rest of the world have at long last become obvious to us. A case in point is the excessive concentration in one's hands of structures with real power and divisions engaged in specific operations. Such a concentration is politically unsafe, as the August coup has demonstrated. Industry has occupational safety rules. Similar rules should be enforced during the development of state structures.

Question: Let me ask a more specific question: what structural changes are under way in the KGB?

Answer: Several directorates and divisions have been disbanded. For instance, the KGB no longer controls Directorate Nine, which is responsible for the protection of top state officials, nor does the government communications directorate belongs to the KGB any longer (incidentally, the latter used to devour about one-quarter of the KGB budget). The military counter-intelligence service and all armed units have been handed to the Defense Ministry. The question of isolating the border guards corps into a separate structure is under study. There is no longer such a body as the Board of the KGB.

One should bear in mind that all these changes are largely politically motivated. An appropriate structure of the KGB is taking shape as agreements are being reached with the republics on the delimitation of functions.

Question: What are the functions of the analytical department of the KGB?

Answer: In principle, they are the same as in the past: providing top officials of the KGB and the state leadership with information and analytical material. True, the list of addressees has changed: it now includes the USSR President and the State Council, the leadership of the republics (they are highly interested in our information) and some other bodies of state authority. In other words, our job is to send out information from the KGB. Before you ask me that question, let me tell you that party and other public organizations are not among our addressees.

Question: Where does the KGB get its information?

Answer: As a rule, we do not gather information ourselves. We receive information processed by functional departments of the KGB, notably the intelligence and counterintelligence services, as well as other structures.

Question: What kind of information does your department disseminate?

Answer: Any information that bears on national security interests. It may be information in the sphere of politics, economics and science.

Question: Have any qualitative changes taken place in the operation of the analytical department as compared with the period preceding the coup d'etat?

Answer: We are certainly faced with making some changes.

Question: What should these changes be?

Answer: Firstly, information coming out of the department should be objective, authentic and socially useful.

Question: Do you have grounds to assert that the department's information did not meet those demands earlier?

Answer: Yes, under the former KGB chiefs it was tendentious to a certain extent and was geared to certain political requirements.

Question: To what extent did the information provided by your predecessor influence President Gorbachev's actions?

Answer: It is impossible to determine the extent of that influence in quantitative terms. If only for the simple reason that our country, unfortunately, lacks what I would call information culture. The staff of the USSR President was a meeting point for several different information channels. These channels were chaotic and distorted---a fact that largely explains the well known mistakes made by Gorbachev. As a rule, only information that came in line with the interests of certain political forces was communicated to him. Monopoly on information, that is, a situation whereby both the intelligence and counterintelligence services are in the same hands and whereby there exist certain personal sympathies and antipathies between the heads of the power structures, made it possible to manage the flow of information directed at the president.

Question: Now that the KGB is being reorganized, what fate is in store for its informants, that is, those squealers who used to inform against one's fellow-workers for decades, who reported "hostile" sentiments and "harmful" pronouncements?

Answer: First of all, let me note that secret services all over the world work with agents. This is natural, for without agents their operations would be impossible. The main question is what methods are employed in the process. One can speak of liability only if a specific agent breached the law. True, I don't think that any documentary evidence can be discovered now to show that agents were at work among, say, the corps of people's deputies or former political opponents. Officially, such operations were against the law and service instructions. This is why all directives and orders were in all probability passed by word of mouth. As for the archives which include informants' cards, they are sealed up now and their future will be decided by politicians.

Further, I can say that the new structure of the KGB does not include the "z" department, or the former Fifth Directorate which monitored public sentiments. This means that the majority of agents involved in the political police structure are now out of business. In addition, in view of the rehabilitation of innocent persons subjected to repression, all cases which passed through that directorate will be reviewed.

And one more point. I would distinguish between the system of KGB's work with agents, and squealing as a social phenomenon that strongly affected our society long ago. Doesn't squealing and spying exist in the staff of each establishment and organization? Didn't we cultivate the image of Pavlik Morozov for decades? In conditions of the totalitarian regime that phenomenon became a way of life, a social disease. This is why you needn't blame the KGB for everything.

Question: To end our discussion on that point, how many informants does the KGB have?

Answer: I'm afraid no one keeps track of the exact figure. I personally don't know. However, relying on my experience I can offer you one indicator, the so-called density of operational activity. When I worked at the Voronezh Aircraft Plant in the 1970s, it totalled one informant per 1,000 employees. It was a defense-related production facility and, naturally enough, the indicator was one of the highest.

Question: My last question is what will happen to the recently enacted law on the KGB?

Answer: I expect it to be revoked, because the structure which that law aimed to legalize no longer exists. Besides, I don't think such a law is necessary. We need other laws: on national security, state secrets, intelligence operations and so forth. Which organizations will perform these functions is a matter of secondary importance.

THE FIRST PLOT TO SEIZE POWER?

By Pavel Antonov, Novosti commentator

"Ladies and gentlemen! Comrades! Do you remember the last conspiracy designed to oust the legitimate authorities in this country? No you don't. So far there have been no such precedents. It is consequently very difficult to qualify the activity of our clients."

Alexander Kligman, defense attorney of Victor Grushko, ex-first deputy chairman of the KGFB, said this at a press conference in Moscow on September 17th. The press conference was given by Kligman and four other lawyers who agreed to be the defense attorneys of the leaders of the abortive August coup: Alexei Galoganov (for ex-Premier Valentin Pavlov), Alexander Gofstein (for Anatoli Lukyanov, ex-chairman of the Supreme Soviet of the USSR); Yuri Ivanov (for ex-KGB Chief Vladimir Kryuchkov); and Yuri Borovkov (for Valeri Bodlin, President Gorbachev's ex-chief-of-staff).

The press conference began with short introductory remarks from each of the five lawyers.

Alexei Galoganov, Pavlov's defense lawyer: The circumstances related to the investigation of the State Committee for the State of Emergency case accord us the right to meet journalists in order to furnish them with first-hand information.

This is also the first press conference sponsored by the Union of Russian Lawyers. It aims to protect suspects who have been arrested in relation to the case of the former State Committee for the State of Emergency. We decided to meet with you because regrettably not all the mass media objectively cover the investigation of this case. We are misquoted in the press. Attempts are made to classify the activity of our clients before the court has passed its judgement, and public opinion is being manipulated.

I would like to request that representatives of the Procurator's Office of the Russian Federation be more attentive to the rights of the defense lawyers and the wishes of our clients and their relatives. I would also insist that nervous tension not be attached to this case. We will not accept any provocative acts against us or our clients.

I am saying all this because on September 10 my client's cell was searched. Pavlov's personal notes and the transcripts of his conversations with his defense lawyer were taken away and returned only on September 15.

The suspects in custody have the right to keep documents and notes related to their case. No one can take them away and become familiarized with them. I demand that the Procurator General of the Russian Federation thoroughly investigate this occurrence because both the rights of my client and my own have been grossly violated.

"I maintain business-like, working relations with by client. We have decided on a line of defense. I am deeply convinced that my client's activity cannot be defined as a crime under Article 64 of the Criminal Code of the Russian Federation, with which he has been charged. On August 20, 1991, my client had a high blood-pressure. The state of his health is also today, unfortunately, a cause for concern. I have filed a request that my client by transferred from his present location. My request has, unfortunately, not been honored."

Alexander Kligman, Grushko's defense lawyer: The crime which our clients are accused of is qualified in Article 64 of the Criminal Code as treason before the fatherland. It means a deliberate action which is detrimental to the sovereignty, territorial integrity, state security and defense capability of the USSR; transition to the enemy, espionage, betrayal of state or military secrets, flight abroad or refusal to return to the USSR, assistance to a foreign state in hostile activities against the USSR, as well as a conspiracy designed to seize power.

This crime is punished by a prison term of between ten and fifteen years, involving the confiscation of the property of the guilty with or without his exile or death penalty with the confiscation of the property. I have quoted the Criminal Code. If you don't object, I will go on.

For lawyers the issues pertaining to this qualification present a certain difficulty, because there are no theoretical definitions or court practice on this score. Up till now we did not need them at all.

Neither the law nor appendages to it provide a legal definition of the word "fatherland." We have to refer to a dictionary, which defines it as one's native land or the country of one's parents or ancestors'. "Treason" is defined as an offense which is detrimental to the country's sovereignty, territorial integrity, state security and defense capability. I ask you: Did the arrested commit any acts to the detriment of the sovereignty, territorial integrity, state security or defense capability of the USSR?

One of the commentaries to this article specifies that a conspiracy constitutes an act aimed at changing the existing Soviet state and social system. I ask you: Did any of the arrested in this case intend to change the existing Soviet system?

I would now like to quote a Textbook on Soviet Criminal Law. It is an old book but no more recent source is available. According to this book, "treason involves treachery towards the Soviet people, the builders of a communist society. It is based on direct collaboration with imperialist reaction fighting against the USSR and other socialist countries with various means." I ask you, gentlemen: Can the activity of the arrested be defined in this manner?

A few words about my client Victor Grushko. He refuses to plead guilty. The man is in his 60's. He suffers from progressive diabetes. In order to survive he needs to take medicine five times a day and is on a special diet.

I talked to the prison physician. He said that such a diet was impossible in this prison. The daily Izvestia, which I respect very much, wrote that the accused "eat the fruits of socialism built in an individual country."

"In Russian pity has always been accorded to the sick and condemned. Some people in this hall laughed when I mentioned my client's disease. This means that this tradition is regrettably passing into oblivion."

Yuri Borovkov, Boldin's defense lawyer: "It has already been stated here that the lawyers have been asked to swear that they won't make public any preliminary results of the investigation. Now that we are allowed to fulfill our professional duty, we have found out that the investigation intends to introduce special clearance arrangements. In our opinion, it is an illegitimate restriction of our rights---a case of secrecy against openness."

There is such a practice. However, regulations on special clearance for defense lawyers have been secretly worked out by the Council of Ministers of the USSR. The Constitution Compliance Committee of the USSR has stated in the most unambiguous terms that those normative acts which are not published shall have no legal force.

Special clearance arrangements also revive special colleges of lawyers. What about the right of the accused to choose a defense lawyer? We came across this obvious violation of the right to defense in the recent past during closed trials of dissidents, religious leaders etc.

And one more thing. What kind of state secret can we talk about if President Yeltsin made legally null and void all the decisions and documents adopted by the State Committee for the State of Emergency?"

Yuri Ivanov, Kryuchkov's defense lawyer: "I'd like to touch upon a problem which is in my opinion of cardinal importance. Yesterday papers wrote with joy that "Gorbachev was interrogated as a witness in this case," that "the President obeyed the law," and so on, and so forth. But Gorbachev was interrogated in the wrong manner. He is not a witness, but a victim. In accordance with the Criminal Code, a victim is a person on whom physical, material or moral damage has been inflicted. The President says that he was isolated in the Crimea and that his space link and other communications were cut off. According to some reports, his wife's arm was paralyzed and she was on the verge of suffering a stroke. This gives one grounds to classify him as a victim.

This is not a circumstance of secondary importance because the evidence given by a victim and an objective uninvolved witness is appraised differently. President Gorbachev has a stake in the outcome of this case. He can be biased voluntarily or involuntarily.

"I will explain why I, Kryuchkov's defense lawyer, insist that the investigation recognize Gorbachev as a victim. At a meeting with the members of the Russian Parliament, Gorbachev said that an integral investigation team would report to him and Boris Yeltsin on the investigative progress. I quote: "we will inform you and the Supreme Soviet of the USSR. We will take a decision..."

So, what do we have here. The President, who is a victim, is informed about the progress of the investigation. The President gives evidence in the same Procurator's Office which provides him with such information. Whether Gorbachev is a victim or a witness, he, too, ought to have been warned about his personal responsibility for making public material used in the investigation.

In the meantime, the top leaders of Russia---Yeltsin, his Vice-President Rutskoy and others---give one interview after another, claiming whatever comes to mind. General Kobets, Defense Minister of Russia, claims that he was on the list of people under Number 6 who were to face a firing squad. Mrs. Starovoitova who is just back from Britain, alleges that she was on the same list under Number 8. No one has ever seen such lists. If top officials continue to mention these lists, I will not be surprised if the investigation finally finds witnesses who saw the lists.

I would also like to draw your attention to the fact that President Yeltsin, Prime Minister Silayev, Deputy Chairman of the Russian Parliament Khasbulatov and Yeltsin's Advisor Burbulis should also be interrogated as witnesses. They claim that on the eve of, should we say, the storm of the "White House" they talked with my client Vladimir Kryuchkov. How come the investigation is not interested in this discussion. One must confront them with my client and interrogate them together. It is one thing to answer questions from indulgent journalists, and something else to answer the questions of trained lawyers.

President Gorbachev, who is the victim in this case, decrees the establishment of a special presidential commission to investigate the activities of the KGB. This has virtually initiated a purge in the KGB. This commission has been created not by the Parliament which has such powers but a victim interested in the outcome of this endeavor. The commission questions people who are expected to testify but are not warned about their responsibility for any false testimony. In a situation like this, when KGB officers are afraid to lose their jobs, slander on a mass scale cannot be excluded.

"And one more thing. I was shocked to read in the weekly Ogonyok that Prime Minister Silayev wanted my client to face capital punishment. He said that he personally would vote only for capital punishment. In no civilized country would a Prime Minister dare to publicly say such a thing about a person who has not yet been found guilty. I must commend the weekly which published my rebuttal."

There followed a question-answer session.

Question: Do you think that the court will pass a fair judgment or will the leaders of the USSR and Russia have it their way? And the second question. Is there at least one perfectly healthy person among your clients?

Answer (Alexander Kligman): No court can be totally isolated from developments in the country. Nevertheless, we hope that a normal and fair judgement is possible. With regards the health of our clients, I'd suggest that the correspondent who asked this question try to get to the prison and see for himself how the arrested look. This would immediately wash the smiles off many faces in this hall.

Question: Is Lukyanov in breach of the law when he refuses to answer questions from investigators?

Answer (Alexander Gofstein): No. The suspect has the right to answer or refuse to answer any questions. The act of testifying is the suspect's right, rather than his duty. In addition the suspect should be presented with the facts, which provide the grounds for the accusations. He can only, after refuting them, furnish evidence on his behalf. My client has not been presented with any of the grounds for the charges.

Question: Which suspects have already pleaded guilty?

Answer: According to the press, only Marshal Yazov has.

Question: Has pressure been brought to bear on any of the defense lawyers?

Answer (Yuri Borovkov): No, we cannot say that it has. The investigation has been conducted correctly, within the law, and all the procedural actions are carried out in the presence of a defense lawyer.

Question: Would you be glad to become known in history as the lawyers who managed to free the putschists?

Answer (Borovkov): I would be very proud if I obtained a "not guilty" verdict for my client.

Answer (Yuri Ivanov): A defense lawyer is very similar to a doctor, who has been called on to see a gravely ill patient. He must do everything in his power to ease the suffering of his client and fulfill his duty to the very end.

Question: Will you request international supervision of the investigation?

Answer (Kligman): Our court system does not provide for such control. We would be happy if foreign lawyers watched this trial very closely. This will provide an additional guarantee of a fair trial for our clients.

Answer (Ivanov): My client is not going to solicit help from any international organizations.

Question: You have mentioned special clearance which the defense lawyers must have. What if they do not get such clearance?

Answer (Ivanov): We will get together to discuss the situation. We may give up the case, which will result in its suspension. The law does not say anything about the possibility of such clearance. As members of the Colleges of Lawyers, we are not going to put up with any act of lawlessness.

Question: Have any of your clients given the order to open fire?

Answer (Ivanov): Do you know for a fact that any of the military did open fire?

(I could not control myself and shouted: Yes, I do. Because on the night of August 21--22 I personally saw a soldier fire from an armored personnel carrier in the tunnel under New Arbat Street.)

Ivanov continuing his answer: The Moscow Procurator's Office is investigating the death of three people in that place. Ask them, if you need details.

By the way, they are also investigating another version, whereby an armed attack on a personnel carrier resulted in the loss of human life. I do not see a direct link between the imposition of the emergency situation and the death of three, undoubtedly fine, young men. There may be endless indirect ties, but no direct connection. For this reason our clients cannot be accused of causing the loss of life.

Question: How long will this investigation last?

Answer: Members of the Procurator's Office said that they will need around three months.

Question: who will pay the lawyers? If the suspects do, then how much?

Answer (Alexei Galoganov): I was hired by my client's family. The sum of my royalties is a professional secret.

Answer (Ivanov): I do not think that it is a secret. Kryuchkov's family paid me an advance of 3,000 rubles. If the process is delayed, I will be paid more.

Question: Will your line of defense proceed from attributing the main guilt to Boris Pugo, the ex-Interior Minister who committed suicide?

Answer (Kligman): Of course it would be easiest to blame it all on the dead. We are sure, however, that our clients would not ask us to use it. The task is either to prove their guilt or to clear them of all accusations. That's all.

Question: Will there be several trials or one?
Answer: I suppose that the cases of the seven members of the Committee will be united, while the other suspects will be tried separately.
Question: What about Lukyanov?
Answer: I can't say. You need to ask the Procurator's Office.
Question for Ivanov: Will you insist on a Kryuchkov-Gorbachev confrontation? What will you do if you request is waived?
Answer: Before insisting on this, I have to become familiar with Gorbachev's testimony. If there are discrepancies between his testimony and the testimony of my client, then the investigation itself ought to confront the two.
Question for Ivanov: Why are you so aggressive? Has the press offended you?
Answer: The press writes many strange things. I have already mentioned one of them---the capital punishment demand. You journalists often fail to notice that you are insulting the dignity of our clients. The statement Genrikh Igityan made in Parliament---that Gorbachev should not have given high posts to the people with such ugly mugs---was broadcast on television and published in the press. In my opinion, such words are unworthy of Parliament and the papers which reprint them.
Question: We know that fourteen people are under investigation in this case. Has someone else been arrested?
Answer: You should ask the Procurator's Office about this.
Question: Your clients are not kept in solitary cells. Who are their inmates?
Answer (Kligman): I have made inquiries about my client's inmates in order to establish that his "neighbors" are not used to pull additional information out of him. My client's inmate is a man condemned for stealing 800,000 dollars at Sheremetyevo Airport.
Answer (Galoganov): On September 10 all my client's personal notes were taken away from him. This is how it happened. First Pavlov's inmate was taken out of the cell. Then Pavlov was ordered to face a wall in the corridor. When he was allowed to return to his cell, the notes were missing. He declared that they were missing. His inmate has never returned. The notes were given back to their owner only five days later, on September 15.

THE METAMORPHOSIS BEGINS

MILITARY REFORM HAS BEGUN?

By Pavel Antonov

"We can say—a radical military reform has got started." With this phrase began the first meeting of journalists with the new Soviet defense minister, Air Force Marshal Yevgeny Shaposhnikov. He was in a civilian suit, felt at ease, often smiled and replied precisely. The USSR has not known of such a young—he is 50—and charismatic defense minister. One of the most removed words from his image is "martinet." By the beginning of the putsch he commanded the Soviet Air Force and was a three-star general. At the peak of the putsch, on the night of August 20–21 we received the news that Shaposhnikov had been arrested for his refusal to obey Marshal Yazov's order. Shaposhnikov began the press conference by answering the question, "Who stopped the putsch?" In the minister's opinion, it was not a military coup, but just a plot of a handful of persons. "The military nowhere changed power, they overthrew nobody. The army did not act against the people, did not break with it."

And yet the Ministry of Defense is now preoccupied mainly with a reform of the Armed Forces of the USSR. And the first problem of the reform is a departisanization of the army. Yevgeny Shaposhnikov for the first time, three days before the announcement about this in a decree of the Soviet President, said that a Military Reform Committee, made up of representatives of all the republics, had been set up at the State Council.

Question: Why before the words "military reform" did you use the definition "radical?" What constitutes its radicalism?

Answer: Above all, the fact that the Ministry of Defense has for the first time supported the idea of becoming a civilian agency. With a definite set of committees—on military policy, military economics, social security. The Armed Forces with their General Staff will similarly be included in the ministry. Military-political structures have been abolished. I think it is understandable how deep and serious such a change is for our country. The period of military service will be reduced from 24 to 18 months. Nor has our army ever known of such openness. The principle of recruitment for it is being changed—though the constitutional provision for calling to military service, with the exception, naturally, of students, remains, a contract system will also be introduced. This means that after a recruit has spent six to eight months at a training center, he will be contracted for further service.

These and other ideas will soon be considered by the Committee on Military Reform and, in the case of approval, they, probably, in October will be submitted to the State Council.

Question: And will the Soviet Armed Forces be reduced?

Answer: Talks on the mutual reduction of armed forces are now being held in Vienna. As a gesture of good will we have already unilaterally cut our army by 500,000 men. I think that in the transitional period it will be further reduced to three million. But this is not the limit for cuts, the process will continue. It is only essential that it be reciprocal.

Question: Are there Soviet nuclear weapons on the territory of Germany? Yes or no?

Answer: No. There is not a single piece of Soviet-produced nuclear ammunition on the territory of Germany. Nor is there a single chemical charge there. Moreover, there are no nuclear charges on the territory of the Baltic republics either.

Question: Are any defense spending cuts being planned?

Answer: Probably it is not the matter of a defense minister to raise the question of reducing the military budget. Quite another thing---the reallocation of expenditures. We shall reduce the main item of expenditures---the purchase of military equipment. But we must increase them for the upkeep of our officers' corps. Spending will also rise after the shift to the mixed principle of recruitment for the army. So that the structure of the military budget will change, but I would not reduce its size.

Question: Is it true that the Ukraine wants to become a zone free of nuclear weapons, and has the question of rebasing these weapons from its territory been raised?

Answer: The Ukraine is preparing for elections, and different, often conflicting statements, dictated by the election struggle, are coming in from there. But when we laid out before our Ukrainian colleagues the calculations as to what a dismantling or physical destruction of the nuclear weapons available there would cost, such demands ceased to resound. And another point. God forbid, of course, that something like a nuclear war should break out---I hope this will never occur---but if that suddenly happens, no territory located between nuclear powers can "sit out" the catastrophe, can save itself.

Question: How could the Baltic states help the early withdrawal of the Soviet Army from their territories?

Answer: Primarily by their leaders realizing the full complexity of the problems connected with this. Until 1994 we shall be preoccupied with the pullout of our troops from Germany. After that we shall start withdrawing from the Baltic. It would help if the Baltic leaders acted as Germany behaves. This can be agreed at an inter-governmental level. Once we have lived together for half a century, there are all the prerequisites for a civilized, legal approach to the solution of this issue too.

Question: Will military reform change the attitude to nuclear potential?

Answer: The Soviet Union is ready to continue reducing strategic offensive nuclear weapons. But even more important now is to start eliminating tactical nuclear weapons---and, above all, on the European continent.

Question: Will the Soviet Union together with armies of western countries participate in joint military programs directed at ensuring global security, such as the SDI? And---who is now being regarded as potential enemy in the Soviet army during maneuvers?

Answer: We have achieved a level where the USSR defense minister is often meeting with his colleagues from other countries. But I want young lieutenants and even cadets to meet as often as possible. If they get acquainted and believe each other now, then when they live till they are grey-headed, take up high positions, become ministers, all the problems of global security will be solved much more easily.

I do not see a potential enemy now. Though, of course, war danger remains, because there exist powerful groupings of armed forces and there are aggressive leaders. Probable enemies may therefore appear too. Local wars cannot be ruled out, nor attempts to solve political issues by force.

Question: Detaching ourselves from election passions in the Ukraine, if nevertheless that republic's parliament decides on creating its own army and subordinating it to the Ukrainian president, not Moscow, will the Center resist that?

Answer: My personal view is as follows---since we are going to live in a single economic and political space, since we have a single airspace, then, I think, we should also agree on a single military space. But neither do I deny the possibility of the establishment of republic-level military formations or national guards. The suggestion of Russia is that such a guard should number up to 3,000 and guard major national installations.

Question: The officers are worried about their social unprotectedness---low wages, nowhere to live...

Answer: It is a painful, difficult question. I have already signed an order to increase officers' money allowance from October 1. The income tax has been abolished. On the whole, the increment will amount to 40 percent of the previous wage. But it is particularly difficult to solve the housing problem. In the Soviet Armed Forces now about 200,000 families do not have apartments of their own. The troop pullout from Eastern Europe aggravates it still further.

And here is what we are doing ourselves. In the military budget there is an item: for capital construction. A large portion of it used to be spent on such things as testing grounds, training centers, airfields and control posts. Much less for the building of houses. From next year we reverse this ratio. There are other ideas. To pay money compensation for officers and expand cooperative house building. Or, say, three years before the discharge of an officer to allot him a plot and render financial aid so that he can build his own house.

Question: Your attitude to the withdrawal of Soviet troops from Cuba, considering that an American military base remains there? What are their number and how soon do you expect to withdraw them?

Answer: The American base is a question of relations between Cuba and the U.S.A. Our military contingent in Cuba numbers up to 10,000. We shall continue negotiations with the government of Cuba on the reduction or full withdrawal of this contingent.

Question: Who has and will have the right and possibility to push the nuclear button?

Answer: Regardless of republics' aspirations, the Center alone must dispose of nuclear weapons. And on this issue agreement has been reached with them. But, of course, presidents of republics must know what type of weapons, in what amount are held on their territories and how they can be used.

Question: Is there a Defense Council in the USSR now?

Answer: No, there is no Defense Council now. But, I think, it has to be restored, including in it primarily the heads of the republics on whose territory there are nuclear weapons.

Question: Will research and development spending be reduced in the army?

Answer: No, I don't think so. Especially as in some scientific military developments, say, under a program resembling Stealth, we have fallen behind.

Question: Will the army be used for resolving inter-ethnic conflicts in the future?

Answer: I shall do my best to prevent it. I asked my western colleagues what the army does when mass disorders start? And found out that the only thing the army can do in this case is to assume the guard of government offices and other major installations. That's all. We must have a law which would clearly lay down what the army can and what it can never do.

Question: This means that troops will be withdrawn from Nagorno-Karabakh and from the territory of Azerbaijan?

Answer: They do not participate in combat actions in Nagorno-Karabakh, Armenia or Azerbaijan. On the borders of the republics, in order to reduce the confrontation, they have set up outposts, but the troops do not use arms.

Question: Will the new Soviet military leadership continue to keep vast territories of the USSR as closed zones for foreigners' visits?

Answer: I believe that many of the "closed zones" should be opened. The civil authorities share this position. On "closed" territories, in "closed" ports and cities most often there is nothing closed at all. And if there is a truly secret installation somewhere, then it is necessary, while opening the city, to retain the secret regime of this installation.

Question: Do you assume that in the New Oath or Manual it will be written that a subordinate may not fulfill the order of a commander if he deems it illegal?

Answer: No, I don't, because then it will no longer be an army. But, I repeat, there must be a law which will clearly determine the aims and functions of the army.

STATEMENT BY THE USSR PRESIDENT AND THE TOP LEADERS OF UNION REPUBLICS

The actual formation of new allied relations between sovereign states was disrupted owing to the coup d'etat, which occurred on August 19--21, 1991. As a result, the country was placed on the brink of disaster.

If current developments escalate out of control, there may be unpredictable consequences both inside this country and in our relations with foreign states.

We would like to state that the abortive coup and the consequent victory of democratic forces have dealt a serious blow to the reactionary forces and to all those factors, which used to hinder democratic change. Consequently we have a historic chance to accelerate radical reform and renew the country.

In these conditions, the legitimate top leaders of the nation, namely, the USSR President, presidents of the republics and chairmen of their respective Supreme Soviets, who are striving to prevent the further disintegration of government structures have agreed that, while awaiting the creation of a new political and state system of inter-republican relations and inter-republican and Union government structures during the transitional period (that is, while awaiting the adoption of a new Constitution and elections to new government bodies, which would be carried out in accordance with it), it's imperative to:

1) Prepare and sign the treaty on the union of sovereign states by all the republics, which so desire, enabling every republic to independently determine the forms of its participation in the Union.
2) Appeal to all republics, irrespective of their declared status, suggesting that they immediately conclude an economic alliance with the purpose of cooperating within the framework of a common and free economic space and of ensuring the smooth running of the economy, supplies to the population and radical economic reforms.
3) Create the following bodies to function during the transitional period:

—A council of representatives of People's Deputies according to the principle of equal representation from the union republic's, with each republic delegating 20 People's Deputies of the USSR and republican deputies, who will be delegated to the Council by their respective Supreme Soviets. The Council of Representatives will be vested with the following tasks---fulfilling legislative functions and drafting a new Constitution of the Union of Sovereign States;
—A State Council consisting of the USSR President and top executive officers of Union republics to jointly resolve the issues of domestic and foreign policies which concern the republics' common interests;
—To create an interim inter-republican economic committee, consisting of representatives of all republics on a parity basis, which would be responsible for the coordination nationwide economic management and the implementation of economic reforms.

Following the drafting of a Constitution, it should be reviewed and endorsed by the parliaments of Union republics. And, finally, it should be adopted at a congress of plenipotentiary representatives of the Union republics.
—To confirm the preservation of all USSR People's Deputies' status for the entire remaining tenure of office.

In this connection, we are asking the Congress to suspend the operation of the corresponding articles of the USSR Constitution.

4) To conclude a defence agreement in accordance with the principles of collective security with the aim of preserving joint armed forces and a common military-strategic space, implementing radical reforms in the Armed Forces, the KGB, the Interior Ministry and the USSR Attorney's Office, with due account taken of the republics' sovereignty.
5) To maintain strict compliance with all international agreements and commitments assumed by the USSR, including issues of arms control and arms reduction, as well as foreign-economic obligations.
6) To adopt a declaration guaranteeing the rights and freedoms of citizens, regardless of their nationality, place of residence, party affiliation and political views, as well as the rights of national minorities.
7) To request that the Congress of USSR People's Deputies support the appeal by the Union republics to the UN on recognizing them as parties to international law and examining the question of their UN membership.

The aforementioned measures, prompted by current developments, must be carried out without delay. Consequently, we ask Congress to adopt a resolution on these issues as soon as possible.

The statement was signed by the USSR President and the top leaders of the Russian Federation, the Ukraine, the Byelorussian SSR, the

Republic of Uzbekistan, the Kazakh SSR, the Republic of Azerbaijan, the Republic of Kyrgyzstan, the Republic of Tajikistan, the Republic of Armenia and Turkmen SSR.

Georgia acted as an observer during the session.

Some republics voiced their suggestions and remarks during the night session, but subsequently withdrew them in the morning.

In connection with a corresponding statement, the deputies have been issued with another statement dealing with the procedure of work, which was also signed by the aforementioned leaders.

SPEECHES AT THE EXTRAORDINARY CONGRESS OF USSR PEOPLE'S DEPUTIES

By A. Obolensky

Speech from Mikhail Gorbachev (Excerpts)

I'd like to make the following statement. As far as my commitment to revolutionary, deep-going changes encompassing all spheres of our society's life is concerned, I've remained the same. I'm still committed to the main choice I made in April 1985. However, I've changed because I've discovered the mistakes and miscalculations made with regards to tactics, methods and actions. First and foremost, I failed to comprehend in due time that at this stage, we should have acted more quickly to get rid of totalitarian structures, which impeded any progress. I was unable to use by authority to unite new democratic forces, which could have completely shouldered responsibility for implementing this line, in full measure. I should have done this in time.

Speech by the Russian President Boris Yeltsin (Excerpts)

The governmental crisis, which has been plaguing the USSR for a long time now, continues to deteriorate. The Union leadership used to act by trial and error for months on end; it didn't have a clear-cut political line, tending to proclaim all sorts of slogans instead. Although those slogans were correct, the national leadership used to hinder their implementation in every way possible. Various agencies and departments, which were totalitarian in essence, had been entrusted with the task of translating reforms into real life. It seems that everything was being done to prevent the destruction of party and state structures. And today the Attorney's Office has more than enough reasons to disband the CPSU (Communist Party of the Soviet Union---Ed.) bodies. People, who had in fact acted as leaders of reactionary forces, were responsible for the implementation of top-priority reforms.

Such an approach led to a profound crisis, disorganizing the life of the entire nation.

The country had no high legislative power or parliament during the putsch. The junta was free to do anything it pleased. On failing to act, the Supreme Soviet gave the junta the go-ahead.

On the whole, the Union Center remained virtually unchanged until recently. It had fallen far behind the entire nation and consequently could no longer understand what processes were taking place all over the USSR. Party apparatchiks continued to play the lead inside the center; and everybody knows what their attitude towards the reform drive is. When it became obvious that party and state structures were losing control over the country, they decided to resort to extreme measures, i.e., violence against millions of people and the country as a whole. They planned to resort to force, in order to plunge the USSR back into the past.

When assessing the causes of the putsch, I will inevitably mention the part played by the USSR President himself. He was not consistent enough in the implementation of reforms; he used to show indecision, and would sometimes capitulate in the face of an aggressive onslaught by the party nomenclature whose rights had been infringed upon. All this served to create a favorable environment for revenge by the totalitarian system. I think that Mikhail Sergeyevich knew the real worth of Yanayev, Kryuchkov, Pugo, Yazov and others.

Let's recall January 1991 when the nation was alarmed to learn that President Gorbachev was veering to the right. He was surrendering his positions one after another. The KGB started playing an increasingly repressive role. The army's participation in the resolution of political problems was being legalized; in addition control over mass media had been toughened. The President didn't take Yavlinsky to the G-7 summit in London, preferring to invite Pavlov instead. And it ought to be mentioned that the Soviet people have felt the results of Pavlov's economic policies or more accurately adventures.

Yes, today we're justified in presenting our claims to Gorbachev. But we shouldn't hold him responsible. The entire country, Russia, first and foremost, has changed a great deal, and so has the President. He has managed to reassess many things. This is a trustworthy step.

For my own part, I have much more faith in Mikhail Sergeyevich today than three weeks before the putsch.

Speech by Engineer-Designer Alexander Obolensky (Excerpts)

After the putsch was crushed, the wind of democratization swept through the corridors of executive power, which had hitherto served as a bulwark of reactionary forces. A realistic opportunity for making a breakthrough in the sphere of economic reform has emerged. This could be implemented by forming a coalition government enjoying the people's confidence.

In these circumstances, leaders of those republics, which had been ready to sign the Union treaty on August 18, have started a complete dismantling of Union government structures on August 26th. Does this mean that they would be more content with a conspiratorial dictatorship than with the preservation of the constitutional order? I don't want to believe this. Maybe it's high time that we stopped regarding the Constitution as a prostitute, amending it according to the whims of the new courtesan all the time? We have put the country on the verge of collapse by our constitutional experiments. Any society must have a basis for stability, law and order! The Constitution determines any government's legitimacy. By desecrating the former, we deprive the latter of any respect, releasing a moral "safety catch" in society, according a moral right to resistance by all means to a share of its members. All civil wars, including the Russian civil war, began when legitimate governments were subjected to violence. In fact, our civil war didn't begin with the October coup, which was regarded by society as an attempt to replace one provisional government with another; it got underway when the Constituent Assembly was dissolved. Yes, the central government has indeed been weakened they can easily deprive us of it, simply by forcing us out of this hall or by killing us off. But we have no right to cede our powers on a voluntary basis. The USSR Supreme Soviet was unable to resist the plotters on August 19--21. Ordinary people joined hands and confronted them out in the streets. And our turn has come today; so, it's our duty to defend the constitutional system. If we fail to retain power, then we must at least show the entire world that it was stolen from us. In this way, at least, we might give people a right to resist the self-appointed "rescuers" of the nation.

Speech by Yevgeni Velikhov, Vice-President of the USSR Academy of Sciences (Excerpts)

Indeed, two events have now occurred. The first event in fact represents a crisis and blow, which has shaken society. And just like every crisis, there are two aspects to it. The first one constitutes a drama and the other represents hope.

At present, this blow may propel us forwards, thereby giving society a chance to traverse a long path. Our task is to accomplish this, with due account taken of current realities.

The first reality boils down to the following---we can speak only about fulfilling the will of independent republics. We should proceed from this premise. At the same time, we should understand that in the future the republics will obviously comprehend that certain centralized functions have to be carried out. This is inevitable and meets republican interests. By the way, all speakers seem to agree on this score.

Consequently we shouldn't raze everything to the ground, as in the future we might have to restore all this from scratch.

Speech by Arkadi Yenenko, Rector of the Novisibirsk Civil Engineering Institute (Excerpts)

The national leadership constitutes the source of our troubles and problems. On the one hand, the country's president should be a politician; on the other, he should be an economic manager, so that he could chart a course towards prosperity with the help of existing national structures. Mikhail Gorbachev is a top-notch politician; at the same time he has proved himself to be a rather poor economic manager. Today all of us are reaping the fruits of his leadership, which has led to a virtual collapse of the Union and the national economy, sending our nation backwards. To deliver protracted speeches about perestroika and our future is one thing, but specific actions are an entirely different matter.

Not only did Gorbachev lead the nation, but he also served as the Party's Secretary-General. In fact, his style of leadership led to the following result---a number of top officials, who were his associates have become embroiled in this putsch. Only an underachiever doesn't know and feel who is your supporter and like-minded person! Mikhail Sergeyevich, you are the Party's General Secretary, its "captain," and you have left the "bridge" at the very time when the party is going through its hardest period, abandoning rank-and-file Communists all the same. That's why I want Mikhail Sergeyevich to draw corresponding conclusions from all this.

But it would be incorrect to blame Gorbachev alone because deputies discussed and approved various programs, and the members of the Supreme Soviet appointed members of the Cabinet of Ministers, taking a direct part in the drafting, discussion and adoption of various laws. Many of these laws are already covered in dust.

If they were to ask me to evaluate the performance of our MPs, I would give them a bad mark for their work.

There are several reasons for this---we have too many MPs; in addition not all of them had to face real election races. And not everyone is ready for this work, which requires basic economic, political and legal knowledge.

It was interesting to watch the latest session of the USSR Supreme Soviet, when some deputies complained that Anatoli Lukyanov had manipulated them as he saw fit, always adopting the necessary resolutions.

Dear MPs!

Anatoli Ivanovich could cast only one vote out of 500, which were your own votes. As a professional teacher, I can assure you that the seemingly easy art of "vote collection" is made possible by painstaking work. The thing is that Lukyanov used to prepare for each session in a very serious manner. And tell me, who of you did the same? Don't be angry with me but such MPs can be counted on the fingers of one hand.

Speech by Alexander Zhuravlev, Deputy Chairman of the Union Council's Commission on Labor and Social Policies (Excerpts)

A Union cannot be created in accordance with those "blueprints" envisaged by the draft Union Treaty. This is not going to be a country or a state. When they say that we'll remain MPs until our term expires, they are deceiving us once more. We shall cease to be MPs a few days after the signing of the Union Treaty, because you can't be an MP in a non-existent country. There is no such country, as envisaged by the draft Union Treaty; such a country simply can't exist.

A territory of one nation can't serve as a territory of another nation at the same time. Neither can a capital of one state serve as a capital for another. That's why the capital of such a state, as conceived by the Union Treaty, can only be located in the town of Novo-Ogarevo.

We should be very careful now. Only we can save ourselves. I completely agree with the statement Deputy Obolensky made yesterday.

How should we deal with our President? This is another matter. I don't exactly know who he is. The final verdict can be passed by the court or, quite possibly, only by the test of time. Everything will depend on his present-day actions---whether he acts as a democrat or as a bureaucrat who is trying to conceal his identity.

I'm a convinced Communist because, in may opinion, the Communist idea constitutes a secular form of Christianity's existence. That's why I'll never discard this concept.

I'm a deeply "religious" person, who deeply respects all believers, regardless of their faith. Ours is a Christian--Moslem country. We are a nation of European-Asian culture and should be aware of this fact.

We should also understand that if they want to divide our country, they may play on both our national and religious sentiments. We should understand all this. Consequently, in our opinion, we should study these proposals rather attentively. We must by no means dissolve the Supreme Soviet---it must fulfill its duty. Consequently we must preserve the Supreme Soviet, revamp it and continue the efforts made to democratize the country. Only then will it be possible to save our long-suffering country, which is still a great state. If we save the country, we'll manage to save ourselves, as well.

Speech by Engineer Alexander Kraiko (Excerpts)

The defense of the Russian parliament and the blood spilled in the streets of the capital constitute the most tragic page of the August events in Moscow. Still this does not represent the entire truth about the coup. We should summon up all our courage and admit that a great number of citizens remained indifferent towards the legitimate President, to the plotters and the Constitution during those suspense-filled days. And this is the most terrifying truth about the events, which took place on August 19--21.

Speech by Writer Olzhas Suleimenov (Excerpts)

In his speech yesterday, the outstanding physicist Yevgeni Velikhov compared the putsch to a blow which has propelled society forwards. According to the laws of general physics, a body can be propelled forwards even by a strong kick. It looks as if, the USSR Supreme Soviet and the Congress of USSR People's Deputies are receiving the same kind of acceleration.

Speech by Academician Dmitri Likhachev, Board Chairman of the Soviet Culture Foundation (Excerpts)

Preserving the Union represents the most important problem today. Its disintegration would cause the catastrophic destruction of all our republics. This should be clear to all those present in this hall; in addition, all Soviet people have to understand this. Every worker and farmer, not well-versed in bureaucratic lingo, and who may not understand such notions as "economic space," etc., must understand this, as well. They must clearly understand why they need the Union. Indeed, people are saying that a common economic space must be preserved. However, they'll fail to convince the residents of Chelyabinsk and Cherepovets of this, because local people want to get rid of their factories and will only cross their fingers if this happens. What they need is food, clean water and fresh air.

People are saying that a collective defense system must be maintained. Still this will hardly convince anyone. The republics would say that they don't want to defend themselves and that they are proclaiming non-nuclear zones on their respective territories. Now that the Ukraine has declared itself a denuclearized zone, other republics are going to follow suit. And then the Russian Federation alone will have to shoulder the entire nuclear weapon burden.

These arguments hold no water. All this could be abolished within a year or two; and by that time our country would have disintegrated, even if we were to adopt the decisions today.

Everything might well be severed. Still there is one thing which can't be changed not even by the Almighty himself. We have to understand this. Our past, history and common culture can't be changed, despite the fact that some Soviet historians would like to control the past, changing it as they see fit. However, no one can accomplish this task.

We have a common culture. The past lives inside the present, and we simply can't do away with it. Indeed, who is Gogol? Is he a Ukrainian or Russian writer? Well he belongs both to Russia and the Ukraine.

If we build a new 1,000-km "Berlin Wall" between our nations, then we'll become a conglomerate consisting of third-rate states---from the political, military and, most importantly, cultural point of view.

Why is our country one of the world's leading powers? Because it has a great, multi-ethnic, culture. That's why we must preserve our traditions, as well as our cultural and scientific heritage. We must preserve our museums, which belong both to one single nation or state, be it an independent one, and to a multitude of states at the same time. We need unity in order to preserve our lead in many fields of culture and science and in sports (for we'll be unable to create a select soccer team if our country splits into 15 republics), provided that all our peoples are guaranteed universal and complete equality. By the way, there are almost 300 peoples, not republics, in our country. And these peoples constitute a major cultural value. All peoples, even the smallest ones, must enjoy equality on a par with great nations.

Declarations of human, cultural and scientific rights must be drafted and adopted.

Speech by Miner Victor Goncharov (Excerpts)

Two and a half years ago the people entrusted us with the destiny of this huge and powerful state. At that time each of us had no doubts about the twisted and deformed nature of the Stalinist system; but we knew nothing about its viability. We were both angry and joyful when we entered this hall. We regarded Gorbachev's perestroika, reforms and democracy as a holiday. But as time passed, resistance, doubts and disappointments would grow continually.

I'd like to touch on the political, moral and human aspects of this issue. As you may remember, some people were goading Gorbachev forwards, while others did their best to hinder any moves he made. In the meantime, he patiently maneuvered between the right and left in a bid to avoid a direct clash between the confronting sides who were ready to destroy each other. And he hindered both those on the right and left. Gorbachev did not try to save himself by any means.

Do you remember who demanded Gorbachev's resignation? Umalatova, Alksnis, Petrushenko, Afanasyev, Yeltsin, party functionaries and democrats alike. For his part, Leonic Kravchuk said during the Vremy news show on August 19, 1991 that this was bound to happen sooner or later.

Some people hated him and continued to do so today, only because he gave too much freedom to everyone. Others hate him for not giving enough freedom. Still others hate him for demolishing the Union. Others hate him for hindering this process. And another category of people hates Gorbachev for the demise of socialism. Others hate Gorbachev because he is committed to the socialist choice.

Indeed, we are living in another country. The people have risen from their knees and have tasted the fruits of democracy. That's why I believe that the people of the republics (states) should determine the form of their participation in the Union only by a new referendum. That is, if the March 17 referendum proves insufficient for this purpose. A qualified majority of those taking part in the referendum should determine precisely the form of participation in the new Union or secession from it. Those republics, whose people decide to create a federation should adopt the Union Constitution also by means of a referendum.

It's high time we stopped deceiving people and manipulating their opinions and emotions. Let's remember the US Constitution's preamble: "We, the people of the United States, in order to form a more perfect Union, establish justice, insure domestic tranquility, provide for the common defense, promote the general welfare, and secure the blessings of liberty to ourselves and our posterity, do ordain and establish this Constitution for the United States of America." Haven't we learned a thing or two from the civilized world ever since the Iron Curtain came tumbling down? One US correspondent said jokingly that our country should add another "S" to its name. "Is it the word `Sovereign'?" I asked. "No, `Sumashedshih' (Crazy)," he answered. I don't think he was interfering into our internal affairs. Regrettably, he was telling the truth and nothing but the truth.

Speech by Writer Yuri Karyakin (Excerpts)

I would like to speak about one of the reasons for the putsch and the reason for its failure. To cut a long story short, I'd like to touch upon the relationship between the two presidents---Gorbachev and Yeltsin.

They have been clashing for nearly four years on end. However, they also cooperated on the creation of the "500 Days" market program and the Novo-Ogarevo agreements. Somewhere in 1987, Gorbachev swore that he'd never allow Yeltsin to indulge in politics again. Unfortunately, he almost kept his word. For his part, Yeltsin pledged that if Gorbachev were wounded, surrounded or found himself in dire straits, he'd come and rescue him no matter what. And, fortunately, he remained true to his word.

But for the "White House" and St. Petersburg, the putsch would have succeeded. Still we should keep the following thought in mind---nobody knows how things would have worked out if Gorbachev and Chernyayev had failed to stand their ground at Foros.

Quite possibly, most of us regarded August 21--22 as the happiest days of all. I myself was overcome with joy. Still I was extremely distressed when I watched Gorbachev's news conference. Forgive me, Mikhail Sergeyevich, but surely you must remember what you said back then. Figuratively speaking, you showed us the same old "compass," which had led us to this defeat, despite the fact that the "ship" had already been "smashed" against the rocks.

However, you changed your mind one day later. Was it a tactical ploy, a political move that had been forced upon you, or was it a genuine gleaning of the truth, which had been brought about by the shocking and harrowing experience you suffered? I can't answer this question today.

I believe, no I want to believe very much that a new Gorbachev will emerge.

Two years ago those present in this hall, or to be more specific, most of us rose in ovation when the "nation! Motherland! Communism!" call was sounded. That was an impressive ovation, indeed. And only an infinitely small group of "renegades" (as they were called at the time) headed by Andrei Sakharov didn't rise to their feet. As far as I can remember, I had that mixed feeling of sadness and horror. Just think of that weird and terrifying union!

And just one more thing. If the coup had succeeded, this congress would have voted for the junta. That's why we must leave our mandates here in front of the entire nation. This will be just about the only way out!

Not a single person here can be trusted. Neither can we trust the minority, which failed to cope with the majority.

LAW OF THE USSR ON BODIES OF STATE POWER AND ADMINISTRATION OF THE USSR DURING THE TRANSITIONAL PERIOD

Article 1. During the transitional period that supreme representative body of power of the USSR shall be the Supreme Soviet of the USSR, consisting of two independent houses: the Council of the Republics and the Council of the Union.

The Council of the Republics shall comprise 20 deputies from each Union republic from among People's Deputies of the USSR and of the Union republics, delegated by the supreme bodies of state power of these republics. In view of the federative structure of the Russian Federation, it shall have 52 deputies in the Council of the Republics. Other Union republics having republics and autonomous formations in their structure shall additionally delegate to the Council of the Republics one deputy from each such constituent republic or autonomous formation. To ensure equality of the republics in the voting in the Council of the Republics, each Union republic shall have one vote.

The Council of the Union shall be formed of deputations from the Union republics from among People's Deputies of the USSR in accordance with the existing quotas and in coordination with the supreme bodies of state power of the Union republics.

Article 2. The Council of the Republics and the Council of the Union of the Supreme Soviet of the USSR shall, by joint decision, make amendments in the constitution, admit new states to the USSR, hear out the President of the USSR on the most important issues of home and foreign policy, approve the union budget and the report on its execution, declare war and conclude peace.

The Council of the Republics shall pass decisions on the organization and the working procedure of the Union bodies, ratify and denounce international treaties of the USSR.

The Council of the Union shall examine questions of ensuring the rights and liberties of citizens of the USSR and pass decisions on all issues belonging to the jurisdiction of the Supreme Soviet of the USSR with the exception of those which belong to the jurisdiction of the Council of the

Republics. Laws passed by the Council of the Union shall come into effect only after their approval by the Council of the Republics.

The supreme bodies of state power of the Union republics shall have the right to suspend on the territory of their republics laws adopted by the Supreme Soviet of the USSR only if they contradict the constitution of the Union republic.

Article 3. For coordinated settlement of home and foreign policy questions bearing on the common interests of the republics, a State Council of the USSR shall be set up on an interrepublican basis. The State Council of the USSR shall consist of the President of the USSR and supreme executives of the Union republics, specified in the Constitution of the USSR. The State Council of the USSR shall work under the supervision of the President of the USSR. The State Council shall itself decide the order of its activities. Decisions of the State Council of the USSR shall have mandatory character.

Article 4. The post of vice-president of the USSR is hereby abolished.

If, for some reason, the President of the USSR cannot any longer discharge his duties (including for health reasons confirmed by a conclusion of a state medical commission formed by the Supreme Soviet of the USSR), the State Council of the USSR shall elect from among its members a Chairman of the State Council of the USSR, who shall temporarily discharge the duties of President of the USSR. Such a decision shall be approved by the Supreme Soviet of the USSR within three days.

Article 5. For coordinated management of the national economy and coordinated implementation of economic reforms and social policy, the Union republics shall form on a parity basis an Interrepublican Economic Committee. The chairman of the Committee shall be appointed by the President of the USSR with the consent of the State Council of the USSR. Supervision of the federal bodies which have defense and security matters, law and order and international affairs under their jurisdiction shall be done by the President of the USSR and the State Council of the USSR.

The Interrepublican Economic Committee and the chief executives of the federal bodies shall be accountable in their work to the President of the USSR, the State Council of the USSR and the Supreme Soviet of the USSR.

Article 6. The status of People's Deputies of the USSR shall be enjoyed by all deputies for the duration of their term of office, including the right to participate in the work of the Supreme Soviet of the USSR and of its bodies.

Article 7. The first session of the new Supreme Soviet of the USSR shall be convened by the President of the USSR not later than October 2, 1991.

For the period up to the beginning of the work of the new Supreme Soviet of the USSR, the present Supreme Soviet of the USSR shall retain its powers and its session may be convened by the chairmen of the two houses.

Article 8. Provisions of the Constitution of the USSR shall remain in effect insofar as they do not contradict this Law.

Amendments in the Constitution of the USSR, adopted by the Supreme Soviet of the USSR, shall come into effect after their ratification by the supreme legislative bodies of all Union republics.

Article 9. This Law shall come into effect from the moment of its publication with the exception of Article 2, which shall come into effect from the moment of the opening of the first session of the new Supreme Soviet of the USSR.

President of the Union of Sovuet Socialist Republics

M. Gorbachev

The Kremlin, Moscow.
September 5, 1991

FOREIGN POLICY FOLLOWING THE PUTSCH

By Alexander Bovin

Boris Pankin began his career as a journalist, eventually working his way up to editor-in-chief of *Komsomolskaya Pravda*. The ups and downs of his subsequent career never let him to forget that a journalist's life is not an easy one. Even though his plane to New York was due to depart in four hours and his office was surrounded by the usual preflight madness, Pankin agreed to meet with this journalist from *Izvestia,* although he gave me one hour instead of the two I requested. "Forgive me," he told me, "I'm in a terrible hurry!" I forgave him.

Bovin: So, now you have entered office. What have you accomplished? Your very first step...

Pankin: First of all, I did not enter this office immediately, but rather, the hall of the collegium. Secondly, I was taken there. Revenko, the Soviet President's chief of staff, took me there and introduced me to the collegium on the President's order.

I remember that I said that I was not going to make any King's speeches and that I wished to ask Vladimir Petrovsky to be the first deputy minister. Then I asked Yuri Deryabin, the head of the department on security and cooperation in Europe, whom I knew from Stockholm and Prague, to become deputy minister.

Bovin: Did you choose these men yourself, or were you "advised?"

Pankin: The choice was mine. I informed Gorbachev and Yakovlev of my plans when the three of us met.

So I entered this office only after the collegium, on August 29. The first thing I did was to summon Petrovsky and Deryabin. The first issue that arose was the issue of the CSCE Conference on the Human Dimension.

Bovin: As I recall, at that time this issue had been almost completely shelved, especially in view of the fact that Yanaev headed the organizational committee.

Pankin: This made it all the more important for us politically to show that events were taking their normal course. We resurrected the idea of the conference, and it actually began on its originally scheduled date.

Bovin: When and how did your collegium disband?

Pankin: One of the collegium members came to me and said that he wanted to move that the collegium disband in order to make my job easier. I agreed with him. When the Extraordinary Session ended on September 4, the collegium was convened and voted to disband.
Of course the media wrote that this was extremely inopportune, but in fact, the disbandment made my life easier and did not create any problems at all.

Bovin: Has the collegium already reconvened?

Pankin: Yes, and it contains new blood. We have invited Olzhas Suleymenov to take a place in the collegium. He is a deputy of the USSR Supreme Soviet and an active member of the Nevada-Semipalatinsk movement. I have already met with him and heard about all of his ideas. Three other men have been named to the collegium in addition to Suleymenov: USSR Supreme Soviet deputy Andrei Sebentsov, corresponding member of the Academy of Sciences Alexei Yablokov, and Vladimir Lukin, who heads the Committee on foreign affairs and international economic ties in the Russian Supreme Soviet.

Bovin: Have any ambassadors left office since the putsch?

Pankin: Four ambassadors were summoned to Moscow before I entered office, and two more afterwards. They were all given the opportunity to reevaluate their positions in view of the changing situation. Leonid Zamyatin opted to take an early retirement; Vadim Loginov (Yugoslavia), Nikolai Uspensky (Sweden), Alexander Baryshev (Guinea-Bissau) and Herman Gventsadze (Ireland) also made up their minds. They returned to their posts to make their farewells.

Bovin: What about Yuri Dubinin?

Pankin: Dubinin will be coming back.

Bovin: Let's just stop and think a bit. Trotsky was the first Foreign Minister of Russia, and Chicherin was the first Foreign Minister of the USSR. do you think that you will be the last Soviet foreign minister?

Pankin: I'm not worried about that, and I think you are mistaken, even if I don't hold this post for a long time. As long as a united country exists then a united foreign policy will exist.

Bovin: But there isn't a united country any longer.

Pankin: There is, and I am confident that there will continue to be. There is the Union of Sovereign States. I spent nine hours at the State

Council yesterday and felt the flood of optimism. I think that the parade of independence, when during the period from August 22 through September 9 eight republics declared their independence, was a sign of protest. They separated themselves from the Union as a source of totalitarianism.

Bovin: And what about as a source of democracy?

Pankin: Perhaps. But I'm talking about something else. When the congress unexpectedly granted them the right to secede, that made the people and their leaders begin to think about how they would live further.

Bovin: So you think that centripetal forces are already at work?

Pankin: I am certain of it. Yesterday's session of the State Council reviewed the food situation in the country as well as other issues which must be rectified before the country can operate as it did in better times. The main goal is to promote informed decision making. Moreover, although a full quorum was lacking at the first Gossoviet session, all the republican presidents and prime ministers attended this past session. In a sense this council is an executive body of power as well as a legislative one.

Bovin: How do you envision the division of power between the Soviet Foreign Ministry and the ministries of the republics (sovereign states)?

Pankin: The already existing Council of Foreign Ministries has received a new lease on life, becoming a useful rather than merely decorative organization. We have offered the ministries a program whereby the Council shall become a legal entity where foreign policy will be hammered out. At the same time, the collegium will become a sort of executive bureau.

Of course, all decisions made by the Council of Foreign Ministries will be reported to the State Council and to the President. We shall meet approximately once a month. We have also decided that our department maintains ties with the republics will be reorganized into the Executive Secretariat of the Council of Foreign Ministries, and will be headed by the deputy foreign minister. In addition to this a committee of permanent representatives of the republican foreign ministries will be created within the Soviet Foreign Ministry. These representatives will act almost as ambassadors, facilitating the coordination of uniform set policies.

Bovin: Don't you think it would simply be easier to initiate an organizational complete restructuring of the system than to try and change the existing psychology, overcome the inertia of the past?

Pankin: Of course, but there is one major problem---it is difficult to separate from the past. Here is the most recent example of this. An agreement was concluded with James Baker concerning Afghanistan, an agreement which everybody approved. But still we were informed that it would have been preferable to hold preliminary consultations with the separate republics before taking any steps.

Bovin: Why didn't this happen?

Pankin: This is an example of the inertia you mentioned. We shall try to conquer it. True, time was an issue here.

Bovin: One could say that Stalin's dream is finally about to come true: all the republics will be represented at the UN.

Pankin: That depends on them. In principle the Congress of People's Deputies has approved this step and now we are waiting to see what the world community has to say. A certain skepticism does exist, and there are fears of precedents being set, yet at the same time it is clear that there is a central power in effect in this country, that there will be a Union of sovereign states and therefore, that our country will remain a permanent member of the Security Council. This is in everyone's interests, especially as this country is a major nuclear power; even Kazakh President Nursultan Nazarbayev has said that they want to resolve this issue with the help of the Union.

Bovin: The Union of Sovereign States...Doesn't the sound of this bother you? A state is sovereign by its very definition. How about one of the other suggested names---the Eurasian Commonwealth of Nations?

Pankin: The name doesn't matter, let's worry about the essence first.

Bovin: Do you see yourself as the foreign minister of a superpower?

Pankin: Yes, and I'll tell you why. I worked as an ambassador for nine years, and with each year that perestroika has existed, I felt more and more like an ambassador from a superpower, right up to my last day in Prague. The world may have ceased to fear us, but it began to respect us. People understand that the fate of the entire world hinges on the Soviet Union.

I think that the media takes a masochistic approach too often, burying our Union and shoving it to the sidelines of world politics too eagerly. I don't agree with this view.

Bovin: How about a few words on your priorities? Perhaps you will list them in order for us?

Pankin: Our top priority is to complete the deideologization of our foreign policy---i.e., Cuba and Afghanistan.

Bovin: Don't you think that it was tactless on our part not to warn Castro about the withdrawal of our brigade?

Pankin: It was simply an oversight on our part.

Our second priority is the economization of foreign activities: our foreign policy should become part of the external economic sphere. On the global scale, this means using all of our diplomatic skill to back up our integration into the world economic structure.

Our third priority has to do with the human dimension, the primacy of international law over national. The individual should always be of greater import than the state, and not the other way around.

Bovin: This is the first time I have heard someone omit disarmament as a priority.

Pankin: But that problem has been resolved in our talks with James Baker. I emphasized two aspects: a complete ban on tactical nuclear weapons and an end to nuclear testing. The Americans have not given their answer yet. A new series of talks is envisaged on strategic offensive weapons. The U.S.A's fears have been allayed concerning the ratification of the signed treaties.

Bovin: What stands in the way of establishing diplomatic relations with Israel?

Pankin: Nothing. It is important that we choose the right moment to establish diplomatic ties so that this step should facilitate peace conference.

Bovin: What about South Africa?

Pankin: South Africa is changing. There will come a time when we will maintain diplomatic ties with that country.

Bovin: Thank you. I wish you luck on all fronts. You have been given a good head start, which you will have to justify.

Pankin: Why do you say "will?" I have already been doing precisely that.

PART II

CONSTITUTION

PREAMBLE

We, the multiethnic people of the Russian Federation,

unified by our historical fate and life on this earth,

in memory of our predecessors, who have preserved and vouchsafed to us their sacred faith in good and justice,

on the foundation of our profound responsibility to the present and future generations of our compatriots,

recognizing ourselves to be a part of world society,

resolute in our determination to affirm freedom, to guarantee human rights and a worthy life, civil peace and international concord, to revive society and make the democratic government of the Russian Federation inviolable —

adopt this Constitution and proclaim it

THE FUNDAMENTAL LAW OF OUR SOCIETY AND OUR GOVERNMENT

SECTION ONE. PRINCIPLES OF THE CONSTITUTIONAL ORDER

Article 1 State Sovereignty

(1) The Russian Federation is a sovereign, federative, democratic, and social state based on the rule of law and consisting of the peoples historically united within it.

(2) The Russian Federation retains supreme rights over its territory and national wealth, independently establishes and conducts its domestic and

foreign policies, and adopts the Constitution of the Russian Federation and the Federal laws, which have primacy within its territory.

(3) The state structure of the Russian Federation is that of a republic.

(4) The government is the official representative of society and expresses its will within the framework of the Constitution. The government as well as its organs and officials, are subject to the will of man and citizen, serve the entire society, and not an element of society.

Article 2 Man, His Rights and Freedoms as the Supreme Value

(1) Man, his life, freedom, honor and dignity, his personal immunity, safety, and other inalienable rights have supreme value. The natural and inalienable right of association is one of the primary guarantees of the rights and freedom of man.

(2) The rights of man are recognized in accordance with the generally accepted principles and standards of international law, and the articles of this Constitution.

(3) Each man exercises within the law his rights according to the principle that all that is not specifically proscribed by law is permitted.

(4) The government is based on the priority of human rights.

The acknowledgement, observation and protection of rights and freedoms, honor and dignity of man represent the primary obligation of the government.

Article 3 Sovereignty of the People

(1) The bearer of sovereignty and the sole source of state power of the Russian Federation is its multiethnic people. The people retain the exclusive right to adopt the Constitution.

(2) The people exercise their vested power both directly and through the system of government organs in the forms and within the limits established by this Constitution.

(3) No element of society, no organization and no individual shall usurp the power of government. The usurpation of government power is a felony.

(4) The representative bodies of the people and other organs, as established by this Constitution, are freely elected by All-Russian, equal, secret and direct ballot.

(5) Citizens of the Russian Federation retain the right, if other means cannot be used, to resist any individual who attempts to forcibly deny or disrupt the democratic constitutional order of the Russian Federation.

Article 4 Political Pluralism

(1) Democracy is based on political and ideological variety and multiple parties.

(2) No ideology shall be established as the official state ideology.

Article 5 Supremacy of Law

(1) The state, its organs and institutions, its officials, citizens and their associations are unified by the law and constitutional structure, acting in strict accordance with the Constitution of the Russian Federation and the Federal laws.

(2) The Constitution of the Russian Federation is the supreme law of the Russian Federation. The standards of the Constitution are directly applied. Laws and other legislative actions that are not consistent with the Constitution of the Russian Federation are not legally binding.

(3) Laws and other legislative actions that are not published officially for wide dissemination are not legally binding on citizens.

(4) The international agreements of the Russian Federation constitute a part of its laws. If international agreements establish rules other than those established by legislation, the rules of the international agreements are to be observed.

Article 6 Separation of Powers

(1) The system of state power is based on the principle of separation of powers into legislative, executive and judicial bodies and a division of authority among the Russian Federation, its component republics, lands, and self-governing territorial associations.

(2) The organs of the state exercise their authority independently, in cooperation and in balance. No government organ may exceed its authority as established by the Constitution or Federal laws.

Article 7 Market Economy

(1) A social market economy, in which freedom of economic activity, freedom of enterprise and freedom of labor, variety and equality of forms of ownership, equal conditions of legal defense, public good and honest competition are guaranteed, is the governing economic principle of the Russian Federation.

(2) The government engages in the regulation of economic life in the interests of society.

(3) Economic relationships are established on the basis of a social partnership between the citizens and the state, the consumer and the producer, the worker and the employer.

Article 8 Social Government

(1) The social policy of the Russian Federation is intended to assure the well being of each person and of the entire society as well as social justice by means of guaranteeing equal opportunities, development of systems of state social services and government social guarantees.

(2) The government protects the labor and health of the people, establishes the minimum wage, assures government support of the family, motherhood and children, invalids and the aged, and establishes pensions and grants.

(3) The government conducts a humane demographic policy, creates the necessary conditions for the development of the social and cultural sphere, supports ecological security and efficient utilization of natural resources.

Article 9 The Federative State

(1) The Russian Federation consists of the republics and lands which have identical rights under the Constitution.

(2) The republics and lands shall be independent to address their own problems, with the exclusion of those relating to this Constitution for the administration of the Russian Federation.

(3) The rights and freedoms of all peoples and ethnic groups are recognized and guaranteed by the Russian Federation.

Article 10 The Russian Federation and the Union (Commonwealth) of Sovereign States

The Russian Federation shall voluntarily, by treaty, enter into a union (commonwealth) of sovereign states in order to manage the common affairs of the union (commonwealth). It retains the right to delegate to its organs a portion of its vested authority. The Russian Federation retains the right to participate in the implementation of common affairs of the union (commonwealth) and to deviate from it.

Article 11 The Russian Federation in the World Community

(1) The Russian Federation is a fully-vested member of the world community, shall observe the generally accepted principles and standards of international law, and strive for universal and just peace, mutual cooperation in the interest of solving world problems.

(2) The Russian Federation shall conduct its own international affairs, establish diplomatic, consular, trade and other relations with foreign states, conclude international treaties, participate in international intergovernmental organizations and associations, and collective security systems.

Article 12 Stability of Principles of the Constitutional Order

(1) The principles of the constitutional order of the Russian Federation are inviolate.

(2) Individual positions as established by the present section of the Constitution, shall be modified solely by referendum of the Russian Federation by means of All-Russian Balloting.

SECTION TWO. BASIC RIGHTS, FREEDOMS AND OBLIGATIONS OF MAN AND CITIZEN

CHAPTER 1 GENERAL CONCEPTS

Article 13

The rights and freedoms of man vest at birth.

Article 14

(1) The basic rights, freedoms and obligations of man and citizen are guaranteed by the Constitution of the Russian Federation. No individual shall deprive man and citizen of his rights or freedoms, nor limit them, except as specified by this Constitution or Federal laws.

(2) The rights and freedoms guaranteed by this Constitution do not constitute all such rights and freedoms and cannot be employed to infringe upon other rights and freedoms of man and citizen.

Article 15

(1) All individuals are equal under the law and before the court.

(2) Equal rights and freedoms of man and citizen are guaranteed regardless of race, nationality, language, color of skin, sex, property or occupation, social position, place of residence, religion, beliefs, membership in public associations or party membership, or other factors.

Article 16

Rights or freedoms as exercised shall not infringe upon the rights or freedoms of other individuals, nor cause harm or damage to the social welfare or the environment.

Rights and freedoms cannot be exercised in a manner intended to forcibly modify the democratic constitutional order nor incite racial, nationalist, social, class or religious hatred nor for hate or war propaganda.

Article 17

(1) Individuals who are not citizens of the Russian Federation, enjoy in its territory all rights and freedoms vested to citizens of the Russian

Federation and shall be bound by all the obligations established by this Constitution, by Federal law and international treaties to which the Russian Federation is a party, with the exceptions specified by these acts.

(2) Foreign citizens and resident aliens requesting political asylum shall be granted asylum by the Russian Federation in accordance with the norms of international law.

CHAPTER II. CITIZENSHIP

Article 18

(1) Every individual retains the right to adopt or reject citizenship in the Russian Federation in accordance with Federal law.

(2) A citizen of the Russian Federation shall not be unilaterally deprived of citizenship.

(3) A citizen of the Russian Federation shall not be exiled abroad.

(4) The Russian Federation guarantees the protection and safety of its citizens abroad.

Article 19

(1) A citizen of the Russian Federation may also retain foreign citizen status in accordance with the laws of international treaties to which the Russian Federation is a party.

(2) The retention of foreign citizen status by a citizen of the Russian Federation does not negate or deprive him of the rights and freedoms, nor relieve him of the obligations, of a citizen of the Russian Federation.

Article 20

(1) The republics and lands of the Russian Federation shall retain the right individually to grant citizenship. All citizens of the republics and lands of the Russian Federation are citizens of the Russian Federation. A citizen of the Russian Federation is a citizen of the republic or land on whose territory he is a permanent resident.
(2) The republics and lands of the Russian Federation are forbidden to limit or proscribe the rights and freedoms, or the obligations deriving from the status of citizenship in the Russian Federation.

CHAPTER III. CIVIL RIGHTS AND FREEDOMS

Article 21

The right to life is a universal right. No individual may be deprived of life arbitrarily.

Article 22

(1) Every individual retains the right to freedom and personal inviolability.

(2) Arrest and other forms of detention shall only be implemented when authorized by a court of law.

(3) Every individual shall have the right to protection from encroachment of his health.

(4) No individual shall be subject to excessive force, or other treatment or penalty which is extreme or degrading to human dignity. No individual may be subjected to medical, scientific, military or other experiments without his free consent.

Article 23

(1) Every individual retains the right to protection from illegal interference in his private life, from violation of the privacy of correspondence, telephone conversations, telegraph and other messages, of his honor and good name.

(2) The collection, storage, use and propagation of information of a personal nature without the agreement of the person involved is permitted only in cases and by procedures established by Federal law.

Article 24

(1) Residential immunity. No individual shall have the right to enter a residence against the will of the persons living therein.

(2) Searches are permitted when authorized by a Federal court of law. In urgent cases, another procedure, established by Federal law, is permissible, whereby the court gives due consideration *post facto* to the legality of the search.

Article 25

(1) Every individual retains the right to freedom of movement, selection of a place of residence within the Russian Federation, with the exceptions established by Federal law.

(2) Citizens of the Russian Federation retain the right to travel abroad as desired and to return without hindrance.

Article 26

(1) Every individual retains the right to freedom of thought, word and unhindered expression of opinions and convictions. No individual may be forced to express his opinions or convictions.

(2) Every individual retains the right to seek, receive and transmit information by any legal means at his disposal.

(3) Restrictions on these rights shall be imposed solely by Federal law for purposes of protecting personal, family, professional, entrepreneurial and state secrets, as well as freedom of conscience and preservation of public morals. The list of information which is classified as state secrets as established by Federal law is a comprehensive list and shall not be construed to include items not specified therein.

Article 27

Freedom of conscience, religion and religious activity is in inalienable right of man. Every individual retains the right to exercise any religion or to exercise none, to select, hold and spread religious or atheistic convictions and to act in accordance with such convictions in a legal manner.

Article 28

(1) Every individual retains the right to free determination of his national origin.

(2) No individual may be forced to define or reveal his national origin.

(3) Every individual retains the right to freely choose a language of communication, to the use of his native tongue and to association with others using his native tongue.

CHAPTER IV. POLITICAL RIGHTS AND FREEDOMS

Article 29

Citizens of the Russian Federation retain the right to participate in the management of the affairs of society and the government both directly and through their freely elected representatives. This participation is embodied in self government, the holding of local and All-Russian referenda, the democratic formation of governmental bodies and other legal methods.

Article 30

(1) Citizens of the Russian Federation shall have the right to elect and be elected in elections of state organs and in elections for governmental positions.

(2) Citizens of the Russian Federation who have reached the age of 18 shall take part in elections. Citizens who have been legally declared mentally incompetent shall not participate in elections.

(3) The laws of the Russian Federation, republics and lands grant the right to vote and be elected to organs of local self government to permanent residents in the corresponding territory who are foreign citizens, as well as stateless persons.

(4) Citizens of the Russian Federation abroad have the right to participate in election of the President of the Russian Federation, Vice-President of the Russian Federation and deputies to the Supreme Council of the Russian Federation.

Article 31

Citizens of the Russian Federation may, after providing official notification to the government, freely assemble peaceably and without weapons, conduct meetings and street processions and demonstrations, and participate in picketing.

These rights may be proscribed in cases as specified by law.

Article 32

(1) Citizens of the Russian Federation shall have the right of association. This right may be proscribed solely by constitutional provision.

(2) Public associations shall be formed openly with official notification of government authorities.

Article 33

(1) Citizens of the Russian Federation shall have the right to personal and public redress by petition to government and public organs and officials.

(2) Government and public organs and officials are obligated to consider such petitions, make decisions and provide a well-considered response within the time established by law.

CHAPTER V. ECONOMIC, SOCIAL AND CULTURAL RIGHTS AND FREEDOMS

Article 34

(1) Every individual retains the right to economic freedom, which is manifested in the right to private property, the right of free enterprise and the right to freely chosen labor.

(2) The right to private property includes the ability at one's discretion to own, use and dispose of one's personal property and other private both individually and jointly.

(3) The exercise of the right to private property shall not infringe on the public good.

Article 35

(1) Every individual shall have the right to support himself by work, which he selects freely or to which he freely agrees, to exercise his working capacity. The freedom to conclude labor agreements is guaranteed.

(2) Every individual has the right to working conditions which meet safety and health requirements, and to payment for labor equal to or grater than the legally established minimum wage.

(3) The State shall endeavor to assure employment for the people by implementing occupational education and training programs, by retraining workers to satisfy social demand, and by guaranteeing payment of unemployment compensation.

Article 36

(1) Vacation time is a right of every worker.

(2) Salaried workers are guaranteed established limits on working hours, weekly days off, holidays, an annual paid leave, and reduced working days for certain occupations and facilities.

Article 37

(1) Every individual shall have the right to accessible, qualified medical care, without direct payment to state or local public health systems.

(2) Paid medical care and medical insurance are permitted.

(3) The Government shall take measures to encourage development of the entire public health system and increase the quality of available medical services. The Government shall encourage activity which tends to protect the environment and improve health, physical culture and sports.

Article 38

(1) Every individual shall have the right to social security in old age, in case of disability, in case of loss of the principal wage earner and in other cases established by law.

(2) Pensions, grants and other types of social assistance must support a standard of living comparable to the officially established minimum standard.

Article 39

(1) Every individual shall have the right to housing. No individual may be subject to arbitrary eviction.

(2) The Russian Federation provides housing through the state and municipal housing fund for the needy without charge or on favorable terms.

(3) The Government encourages the construction of housing and, will establish material and legal conditions in support of such rights.

Article 40

(1) Primary education is obligatory and free.

(2) Every individual shall have the right to free secondary and higher education at state educational institutions.

(3) Private education is permitted.

Article 41

(1) Every individual shall have the right to freedom of artistic, scientific and technical creativity. The freedom of creativity, research and teaching of intellectual property and author's rights are protected by law.

(2) Every individual shall have the right to participate in cultural life and to use cultural institutions.

Article 42

(1) Every individual, regardless of his position, shall have the right to recognition of his individual legal rights.

(2) Every individual retains the right to use all legal means to defend his rights and freedoms. Every individual has the right, independently and by legal means, to respond to violations of rights, and to defend his interests from threats and encroachments.

(3) Every individual is guaranteed the right to professional legal assistance to protect his rights in all institutions. In cases where provided for by law, legal assistance is provided free.

(4) Independent public associations are operated to provide qualified legal assistance from professional lawyers and other volunteer associations of lawyers, as well as individuals, empowered to perform legal duties.

(5) The Russian Federation guarantees every individual a legal defense of his rights and freedoms. Resolutions and other actions or failures to act by government and public organs, institutions and officials in a manner that violates rights and freedoms make such individuals and institutions subject to legal action.

(6) Every individual shall have the right to full compensation by the state for damage to health, as well as material and moral injury, attributable to illegal decisions and actions or failures to act by state and public organs, institutions and officials in the execution of their duties.

(7) When the intragovernmental means for legal protection have been exhausted, every individual may appeal to international legal-services organs, following the procedures established by international agreements to which the Russian Federation is a party.

Article 43

(1) Every individual shall have the right to a review of his case by a legally-established competent, independent and impartial court.

(2) An accused is innocent until his guilt is proven in the manner prescribed by law and established by a legally-binding court decision. An accused is not obligated to prove his innocence.

(3) The right of a person who has been detained, arrested or accused to employ the services of a lawyer at any time shall not be abridged.

(4) Every individual shall have the right to review a legal decision in the manner established by Federal law.

(5) No individual may be arrested twice for the same offense.

Article 44

(1) No individual is obligated to testify against himself, his wife or close relatives, as defined by law.

(2) Evidence obtained illegally shall not be admissible.

Article 45

(1) A person accused of committing a crime has the right to trial before a court with a sitting jury, except for cases specified by Federal law.

Article 46

(1) No *ex post facto* law that establishes or expands legal liability shall be legally-binding. No individual shall be liable for actions that were legal

during the period in question. If the penalty for a crime is abolished or reduced in the period following the commission of a crime, the new law shall be legally-binding.

(2) No individual shall be tried or punished on the basis of a law that has not been officially and openly disseminated.

Article 47

(1) Government and public organs, institutions and officials are obligated to provide every individual with the access to documents directly concerning his rights and freedoms.

(2) The procedure for allowing the accused access to relevant court documents is established by Federal law.

Article 48

(1) The Russian Federation Commissioner of Human Rights and his local representatives are charged with supervision and verification of human rights and the conditions for their protection.

(2) The Russian Federation Commissioner of Human Rights is nominated by the Russian Federation Supreme Council for the term of the Russian Federation Supreme Council, is subordinate to it, and has the same immunity as that of deputies of the Russian Federation Supreme Council.

(3) The commissioner shall have the right to investigate, on his own initiative or in response to complaints, the actions of administrative organs or officials involving violations of human rights, and to stimulate action in representative, administrative or juridical organs.

(4) The status of the Russian Federation Commissioner of Human Rights and his services are regulated by Federal laws.

(5) The republics and lands of the Russian Federation may also nominate their own Commissioners of Human Rights or organs with the same functions. Temporary proscription of rights and freedoms is permitted only in case of emergency, in accordance with the procedures and within the limits established by this Constitution and Federal laws.

CHAPTER VII. DUTIES

Article 50

Each person bears constitutional obligations that must be fulfilled for the normal development of society.

Article 51

(1) Every individual in the Russian Federation shall be obligated to obey the Constitution and other laws of the Russian Federation, to respect the rights, freedom, honor and dignity of other persons.

(2) Ignorance of an officially published law does not absolve the individual of the obligation to obey said law.

(3) Execution of a manifestly illegal order does not absolve the individual from liability for his actions.

Article 52

Every individual is obligated to preserve nature, conserve its riches, and improve the environment. Failure to follow established natural conservation standards is forbidden by law.

Article 53

(1) Every individual is obligated to seek the preservation of historical and cultural heritage, and the preservation of memorials to history and culture.

(2) The list of specially-preserved memorials to history and culture is established by law, as well as by the decision of local government organs.

Article 54

Every individual shall be obligated to pay taxes and duties in the manner and amounts established by law, or by the legally founded decisions of local governmental organs.

Article 55

(1) The defense of the Nation is a duty of citizens of the Russian Federation.

Citizens of the Russian Federation shall perform military service within the limits and in the forms established by Federal law.

(2) If military service violates the religious or moral principles of a citizen, performance of alternate civil duties as established by Federal law may be performed in lieu of such service.

SECTION THREE. CIVIL SOCIETY

CHAPTER VII. ECONOMIC PRINCIPLES OF CIVIL SOCIETY (PROPERTY, LABOR, ENTERPRISE)

Article 56

(1) The right of private and public property is recognized. The right to own property vests to individuals, their associations, and the state.

(2) The law may specify the exclusive right of the Russian Federation, the republics and lands to certain objects of property and types of economic activity.

(3) All owners are equal under the law and have equal legal rights.

Article 57

(1) Property is inviolable.

(2) No individual shall be deprived of his property arbitrarily.

(3) Expropriation of property is permitted only for purposes of public necessity as suitably substantiated and defended in accordance with the conditions, procedures and limits established by law, and with just and timely compensation.

Article 58

(1) The land and its minerals, water, the plant and animal worlds and the continental shelf shall not be used against the interests of the people living within the corresponding territories.

(2) All natural resources are to be conserved and rationally used.

Article 59

(1) Individuals, their associations, and the State may own land. Real estate and its uses are regulated by law.

(2) Land users shall be obligated to preserve the land and increase its fruitfulness. Rights to land shall exclude:

a) improper use or neglect of agricultural land;

b) predatory and incompetent use of land in a manner damaging to its fertility and the environment;

c) the concentration of land in the hands of individuals above the legally-established limits.

Article 60

(1) Labor is exercised freely. Forced labor is forbidden, with the exception of cases established by the international agreements to which the Russian Federation is a party.

(2) The right to strike shall be recognized. Strikes are forbidden in cases where they pose a threat to life or health. Other limitations on the right to strike are established by law.

Article 61

The State defends the interests of the consumer and supports the actions of societies protecting the rights of consumers. Consumers shall have the right to full compensation as provided by law for losses incurred at the hands of producers of goods and services, trade, advertising and other organizations.

Article 62

(1) The Government guarantees the freedom of free enterprise. The procedures, types and forms of enterprise are determined by law.

(2) Political parties shall not engage in business activities with the exception of individual forms specifically permitted by law.

(3) Monopolistic activity, having the purpose of or possibly resulting in the prevention, limitation or elimination of competition, shall be forbidden.

(4) Business activities of foreign organizations and citizens, as well as persons without citizenship, is permitted on the territory of the Russian

Federation. The conditions and procedures of such activity, including guarantees on foreign investments, are established by Federal law.

CHAPTER IX. PUBLIC ASSOCIATIONS

Article 63

(1) Public associations include labor unions, political parties, public organizations, mass movements, religious and other public associations.

(2) Unconstitutional acts and actions, or inaction of government organs leading to illegal proscription of the activities of public associations, the creation of a one-party political system, or the establishment of individual public associations, are forbidden.

Article 64

(1) Labor unions for the protection of the socioeconomic rights and legal interests of workers, as well as protection and improvement of working conditions, are created and act freely. The rights of workers to join or not to join unions, to freely to resign from them, and likewise the right of union organizations to combine and to join international unions, are guaranteed.

(2) Unions represent their members in collective agreements, and may engage in any other activity not forbidden by law.

(3) No union has exclusive right of association nor representation of all workers of an enterprise, industry, or all workers engaged in a given type of activity.

Article 65

Business owners may create associations to defend their socioeconomic rights and legal interests, in cooperation with unions and governmental organs.

Article 66

When necessary and within the limits established by law, chambers, unions, colleges and other private corporations may be established for purposes of engaging in professional activities. Said corporations may be assigned certain governmental rights.

Article 67

(1) Political parties facilitate the manifestation and expression of the political will of society, participate in the elections of representative organs, and, through their elected representatives, in the formation and activity of duly-vested organs. Political parties influence the policies of the government exclusively by legal means. Said parties engage in such activities without hindrance within the framework of the Constitution and other laws of the Russian Federation. Such activities can only be proscribed by court order.

(2) The internal organization and activities of public associations must be consistent with democratic principles.

(3) Political parties, mass movements and other public associations that propagandize race, nationalistic, social and religious hostility and hatred, and those calling for violence and violent overthrow of the constitutional order, are forbidden. Such activities can only be outlawed or proscribed by court order.

(4) The decisions of party organizations shall not be binding on state organs and institutions, enterprises, their employees in the performance of their service or production duties. Organizational structures of political parties shall not be formed in the Armed Forces or militarized formations, in state organs, at state enterprises, institutions or organizations.

Article 68

(1) Public associations have the right to own solely such property, and to engage only in such activities, as are appropriate to their established purposes and tasks.

(2) Public associations are legal entities.

CHAPTER X. RELIGION AND RELIGIOUS ASSOCIATIONS

Article 69

(1) Religion and religious associations are separate from the state.

(2) All religions and religious associations are equal under the law.

(3) The state is secular and assigns no preference to any religion or to atheism.

(4) The State guarantees unhindered legal activity of religious associations.

Article 70

Religious associations, registered in the established legal manner, manage their internal affairs independently. Such associations have the rights of legal entities, may freely own, use and dispose of the buildings, structures, charitable and other funds and other property.

CHAPTER XI. EDUCATION, SCIENCE AND CULTURE

Article 71

(1) Education, science and culture are free. Educational institutions, scientific and cultural institutions shall have the right of independent organization and activity. Higher and secondary educational institutions are autonomous.

(2) The State educational system is secular in nature.

Article 72

Institutions and persons involved in education are obligated to facilitate the education of man as a free, moral, cultured individual, who respects the Constitution of the Russian Federation, as well as the dignity, rights, freedom and legal interests of other people, and is responsible for the preservation of the natural and cultural environment.

Article 73

(1) Public associations and individual persons shall have the right to form educational, scientific and cultural, public health and sports and vacation institutions and to manage such within the constraints of the law.

(2) The State shall maintain various forms of education, develop free schooling, and endeavor to assure equal access based on the ability of each individual, and encourage self-improvement.

Article 74

(1) The State shall encourage public support of science, providing conditions for the development of basic scientific research.

(2) Associations of scientists (academies, societies, etc) are an element of civil society and shall not have administrative control of scientific research activity.

Article 75

The Government shall support the preservation and protection of intellectual and artistic heritage, the augmentation of cultural values, encourage the activity of organizations and persons cooperating in the development of culture.

CHAPTER XII. THE FAMILY

Article 76

(1) The family is the natural basic cell of society. The family, marriage, motherhood, childhood and the aged are under the protection of the society and the government.

(2) Marriage is based on a free agreement between and equality of the partners.

Article 77

(1) Parents shall be obligated to support their children until they reach legal age. Parents have the responsibility for the education and physical development of their children.

(2) The State and society encourage the support and education of orphans and homeless children, and encourage charitable activity for the benefit of children.

Article 78

(1) Children are equal under the law, regardless of the origin and civil status of their parents.

(2) A child retains the right to express opinions, the right of free thinking, conscience and religion.

(3) The State grants a child and his parents or legal guardians the right to select any legal form or type of education for children in accordance with their convictions.

Article 79

Adult children shall be obligated to support their parents.

CHAPTER XIII. MASS INFORMATION MEDIA

Article 80

(1) The mass media are free. Censorship is forbidden.

(2) The mass media are founded by citizens, public associations, State organs and organizations.

(3) Monopolies of the mass media are forbidden.

(4) Arrests or confiscation of information materials and equipment for their production and transmission are permitted solely be a court order.

Article 81

Political parties, other public associations retain the right on an equal basis to utilize state radio and television.

SECTION FOUR. THE FEDERAL SYSTEM

CHAPTER XIV. COMPOSITION AND TERRITORY OF THE RUSSIAN FEDERATION

Article 82

(1) The Russian Federation consists of the republics and lands whose territories comprise the unified territory of the Russian Federation.

(2) The constitutional structure of the republics and lands shall be consistent with the Constitution of the Russian Federation.

(3). A republic or land consists of self-governing territorial entities and their voluntary associations, including those formed on the basis of national autonomy (national oblasts, okrugs, etc.). Such republics or lands may be granted additional autonomous rights depending on their specific national composition as well as other factors. The territorial structure of the republics, and lands is established and regulated by their constitutions and other laws, considering the wishes of the residents.

(4) A State, upon adoption of this Constitution, may be included in the Russian Federation in accordance with the will of its population.

Article 83

(1) Any modification to the composition and borders of the Russian Federation requires ratification by the Russian Federation Supreme Council. The territory of the Russian Federation cannot be modified without the agreement of the people, expressed through a referendum.

(2) The international agreements to which the Russian Federation is a party concerning the acquisition or concession of territory are ratified in the manner provided for by amendment of this Constitution. Treaties refining the locations of its borders must be ratified in the usual manner. If a change in a border involves the territory of a republic or land, its agreement is required for ratification of the treaty.

(3) The borders between the republics (lands) may be altered upon agreement between such republics and the agreement of the residents of the territories subordinate to them.

Article 84

(1) The population of a portion of a republic, land or contiguous portions of several republics or lands may establish form a new republic or land. On the initiative of the number of residents established by Federal law, the voters of the Russian Federation Supreme Council, after consultation with the legal assemblies of the republics or lands involved, organize a referendum in the relevant area. The new republic or land is formed by Federal law in a compact territory, the majority of whose voters have voted in favor of establishment of the new republic or land.

(2) A republic or land may, upon decision by 2/3 of the total number of voters, nullify its existence and become a part of one or more of the adjacent republics or lands. The referendum on this question is organized by the

Legislative Assembly of the republic or land. If, in spite of the presence of a legal initiative, the Legislative Assembly of the republic or land does not organize a referendum, this process will be carried out in the established manner by the Russian Federation Supreme Council. If the republic is abolished, the mandate of its representative in the Federal Council of the Russian Federation is terminated.

(3) A territory, under the proper conditions, may take on the status of a republic or land if it is able to exercise the rights and obligations defined by the Constitution of the Russian Federation, and participate in the maintenance of Federal organs and institutions. This issue is resolved by each of the houses of the Russian Federation Supreme Council.

CHAPTER XV. AUTHORITY OF THE RUSSIAN FEDERATION, REPUBLICS AND LANDS

Article 85

(1) The authority of the Russian Federation includes

a) adoption and amendment of the Russian Federation Constitution, and verification of constitutional observation.

b) acceptance of new republics and lands for incorporation into the Russian Federation

c) citizenship in the Russian Federation.

d) legislation concerning the Federal government organs.

e) Federal property and its administration.

f) the armed forces and national security, the manufacture of armament, weapons, nuclear devices, narcotics and their use.

g) establishment of the basic Federal legal principles; regulation of customs, currency, credit, the monetary commission, management of Federal economic services, including Federal banks and the Federal reserve system.

h) Federal taxes and duties; determination of general principles of taxation in the republics and lands; the Federal budget;

i) conflicting federal law;

j) foreign policy and international relations of the Russian Federation;

k) borders, territorial waters, economic zone and continental shelf;

l) criminal and criminal-procedural law, amnesty and pardons;

m) Federal power systems, nuclear power engineering, fissionable materials; Federal transportation, railroads and communications; space activities;

n) standards and standard time; official statistical accounting;

o) other powers related to the Constitution of the Russian Federation and the administration of Federal government organs.

(2) The republics and lands participate in the execution of Federal powers within the limits and in the forms established by this Constitution and the laws of the Russian Federation.

Article 86

(1) The authority of the Russian Federation, republics and lands includes:

a) the guarantee of human rights and freedoms of citizens, law and order, public safety;

b) civil, commercial, labor, family, financial, administrative, civil-procedural and administrative-procedural law, legal regulation of intellectual property;

c) the judicial system, the legal profession, notaries;

d) natural resources of statewide significance, principles of utilization of natural resources, preservation of the environment, historical and cultural monuments, national parks, preserves and game reserves;

e) education, science, culture; physical culture and sports;

f) public health and social security;

g) citizenship in the republics and lands;

h) quarantine, industrial catastrophes and accidents;

i) civil service;

(2) With regard to the areas listed in (1) of this article, the Russian Federation issues laws relating to the authority of the republics and lands. The republics and lands are authorized to issue laws relating to these areas as well, if the Russian Federation has not exercised its rights of legislation. If the laws of a republic or land do run counter to the Federal law, the Federal law has precedence.

Article 87

(1) The authority of the republics and lands includes:

a) adoption and amendment of constitutions and laws of the republics and lands, and verification of their observation;

b) formation and organization of the activity of governmental organs within the republic or land;

c) legislative initiative in Federal organs;

d) participation in accordance with this Constitution in the formation and activity of the Russian Federation Supreme Council;

e) control of republic or land property; programs of economic, social and cultural development of the republic or land;

f) the budget of the republic or land; local taxes and duties; off-budget funds;

g) territorial subdivision of the republic or land;

h) international relations, except those under the exclusive authority of the Russian Federation;

i) natural resources with the exception of those mentioned in article 93 of this Constitution;

j) protection of the ancestral habitat of small populations and ethnic societies, creation of conditions for national, economic, cultural and linguistic development of all peoples;

k) civil laws;

l) awards and honorable ranks of the republics and lands;

m) other powers, if not withheld or excluded by the articles of this Constitution.

(2) The republics and lands may, within their areas of authority, enter into mutual agreements that are consistent with the provisions of this Constitution.

Article 88

(1) The Russian Federation, by agreement with a republic or land, may cede to the republic or land a part of its authority.

(2) A republic or land, by agreement with the Russian Federation, may cede to the Russian Federation a part of its authority.

Article 89

(1) The Federal laws and other acts of the Russian Federation in the territory of a republic or land are executed by the governmental organs of the Russian Federation, the republic, or the land in the manner established by Federal law.

(2) Legal documents, issued by organs and institutions of the republic or land within their authorized areas, are recognized as valid throughout the territory of the Russian Federation.

Article 90

(1) the Russian Federation, the republics and lands recognize a mutual responsibility.

(2) If a republic or land violates the provisions of the Russian Federation Constitution or the Federal laws and thereby creates obstacles to the normal

activities of the Russian Federation as a whole, the Russian Federation Supreme Council, by decision of the Constitutional Court of the Russian Federation, may obligate the republic or land to pay compensation for damages, occurring as a result of the violation of the Constitution of the Russian Federation and the Federal laws.

(3) Illegal damage incurred by a republic or land at the hands of organs of the Russian Federation are to be compensated from the budget of the Federation by decision of the Russian Federation Supreme Council following a decision by the Russian Federation Constitutional Court.

CHAPTER XVI. OFFICIAL LANGUAGES

Article 91

(1) The official language of the Russian Federation shall be the Russian language. It is to be used in all government organs and institutions.

(2) Each republic or land may independently establish its own official language, which is used in its organs and institutions along with the official language of the Russian Federation.

SECTION FIVE. SYSTEM OF STATE POWER

CHAPTER XVII. THE SUPREME COUNCIL OF THE RUSSIAN FEDERATION

Article 92

The Supreme Council of the Russian Federation -- the Federal parliament -- is the highest representative and only legislative organ of the Russian Federation.

Article 93

(1) The Russian Federation Supreme Council consists of two Chambers: the State Duma and the Federal Council. Both Chambers are elected simultaneously for terms of 4 years.

(2) The State Duma consists of 300 deputies, elected by the citizens of the Russian Federation in territorial elective districts in proportion to the number of voters in each district.

(3) The Federal Council includes three deputies from each republic and land, elected by their citizens.

(4) Any citizen of the Russian Federation who has attained the age of 18 years and has the right to vote may be elected as a deputy to the Russian Federation Supreme Council. No individual may be simultaneously a deputy to both Chambers.

Article 94

The Russian Federation Supreme Council:

a) formulates laws on questions related to the authority of the Russian Federation.

b) adopts resolutions concerning the conduct of referenda in the Russian Federation -- All-Russian National Voting;

c) accepts new republics and lands for incorporation into the Russian Federation;

d) adopts the Federal budget of the Russian Federation and monitors its execution, incorporates changes to the budget, establishes Federal taxes and duties, adopts resolutions concerning Federal loans, economic and other assistance; monitors the monetary commission;

e) upon request by the President of the Russian Federation, grants its consent for the designation of the President and members of the Russian Federation Council of Ministers, the Russian Federation State Secretary, the State Advisors of the Russian Federation, monitors the activity of the executive power, and resolves questions of confidence in the Russian Federation Council of Ministers;

f) upon request by the President of the Russian Federation, appoints judges for the Constitutional Court of the Russian Federation, the Russian Federation Supreme Court and the Superior Court of Arbitration, as well as other Federal judges, the President of the Russian Federation Central Bank and the Prosecutor General of the Russian Federation.

g) elects and recalls the Russian Federation Commissioner of Human Rights, the Chairman and members of the Russian Federation State Treasury.

h) Discharges the President of the Russian Federation, the Vice President of the Russian Federation, as well as the officials listed in sections e) and f) of this article in the events and manner prescribed by this Constitution;

i) ratifies and rejects international agreements of the Russian Federation, including inter-governmental agreements relating to the Union (Commonwealth) of Sovereign States;

j) awards state honors, establishes honorable ranks of the Russian Federation and special ranks;

k) issues acts of amnesty;

l) adopts resolutions concerning the announcement, continuation and termination of emergency states;

m) exercises the authority granted by this Constitution.

Article 95

The Supreme Council of the Russian Federation retains the right to demand, acquire and study any information and documentation from any state organ of the Russian Federation and any official.

Article 96

(1) The Supreme Council of the Russian Federation is a permanently standing organ.

(2) By law the Supreme Council of the Russian Federation convenes on the Tuesday four weeks following elections. The authority of the previous Supreme Council of the Russian Federation terminates on this date.

(3) The activities of the Supreme Council of the Russian Federation are conducted as provided for in this Constitution and the Rules of the Chambers.

(4) If the term of authority of the Supreme Council of the Russian Federation concludes during an state of emergency, the Supreme Council of the Russian Federation adopts a resolution to extend its authority in conjunction with the declaration of the state of emergency.

(5) Elections are held on the second Sunday of March in the year when the term of authority of the Supreme Council of the Russian Federation is complete. The election campaign begins 3 months before the date of the elections.

Article 97

(1) Each Chamber elects its own Chairman, deputy, and adopts its own rules.

(2) The Chambers establish permanent and temporary commissions from the deputies.

(3) Joint committees may also be established by resolution of the Chambers.

(4) The Chambers, committees and commissions study the proposed laws and other acts of the Supreme Council of the Russian Federation, verify the observation of laws, and perform parliamentary investigations and conduct hearings.

(5) The officials and citizens are obligated to appear before the Supreme Council of the Russian Federation, the Chambers, committees and commissions when called, to provide the necessary materials and documents in the established times. Violation of this requirement is punishable by law. The recommendations of the Chambers, committees and commissions are to be reviewed immediately and the results announced.

(6) Each Chamber, regardless of the number of deputies present, shall function as a commission of the whole Chamber in order to discuss proposed laws and other questions without the right to adopt laws and other resolutions other than procedural matters.

Article 98

(1) The right of legislative initiative in the Supreme Council of the Russian Federation belongs to its deputies, commissions and joint committees of the Chambers, the President of the Russian Federation, the Constitutional Court of the Russian Federation, the legislative organs of the republics and lands of the Russian Federation, and also groups of voters numbering at least 300,000

(2) The Chambers consider proposed laws and make decisions separately.

(3) A proposed law is submitted to the State Duma. A proposed law, considered and adopted by the State Duma, is considered by the Federal Council.

(4) A law is treated as adopted if the majority of the elected deputies of both Chambers have voted for it.

(5) In the event of a disagreement between Chambers, a compromise commission of the Chambers is established on an equal basis. The compromise proposed law is once more considered by each of the Chambers. If no agreement is reached, the proposed law is considered defeated and cannot be resubmitted for one year.

(6) Laws adopted by the Supreme Council of the Russian Federation are signed and officially published by the President of the Russian Federation within 14 days after the day of adoption. Up to this point, the President of the Russian Federation retains the right to return the law with his objection to the Supreme Council of the Russian Federation for reconsideration. If upon reconsideration the law is adopted by a two-thirds vote of the deputies in each Chamber, the President of the Russian Federation must sign and publish the law within 7 days.

(7) A law goes into force 3 or more days after its publication.

Article 99

(1) Joint sessions of the Chambers are convened to hear addresses of the President of the Russian Federation and reports of the government, to adopt the Federal budget in case of disagreements between the Chambers, to announce emergency states, and also upon decision by both Chambers in other cased not related to the consideration and adoption of laws.

(2) Joint sessions are chaired by the chairmen of the respective Chambers.

Article 100

(1) A Deputy of the Supreme Council of the Russian Federation has the right:

a) to introduce proposed laws and suggestions for advancement of said laws;

b) to question orally or in writing any organ or official of the Russian Federation. The organ or official to whom the question is directed must answer orally or in writing to a session of the Supreme Council of the Russian Federation, the Chambers, committees, commissions within the period established by law;

c) to address the Supreme Council of the Russian Federation and the Chambers on questions listed in the agendas as prescribed by law;

d) to nominate candidates, including himself, for elected positions in the Chambers, the Supreme Council of the Russian Federation, the commissions and joint committees, and also for the position of Commissioner of Human Rights of the Russian Federation, Chairman and member of the State Treasury of the Russian Federation.

e) to request that any official, citizen be called before the Supreme Council of the Russian Federation, its Chambers, committees and commissions, as well as other rights specified in this Constitution and the Federal laws.

(2) During his term of office a deputy is barred from occupying any other position in state service or any other service, and from engaging in business activity.

(3) A deputy receives payment and compensation for his expenses in accordance with the law, and is barred from receiving any other regular compensation.

(4) A deputy has the right of immunity. A deputy cannot be detained without the agreement of the Chamber, except in cases of detention for a serious crime, arrested, subjected to search, or measures of administrative investigation, brought before a court, or arrested on a criminal charge. This immunity extends to correspondence, communications facilities used by the deputy, and to documents belonging to him. The Procurator General of the Russian Federation will make the appropriate representation to the Chamber.

(5) State organs and officials are obligated to cooperate with deputies in the performance of their duties.

CHAPTER XVIII. THE PRESIDENT OF THE RUSSIAN FEDERATION

Article 101

(1) The President of the Russian Federation is the highest official of the Russian Federation. He exercises executive power, and represents the Russian Federation in its domestic and foreign relations.

(2) Only a citizen of the Russian Federation of at least 30 years of age, having the right to vote, may be elected as President of the Russian Federation.

(3) The President of the Russian Federation cannot function as a deputy, or occupy any other post, or a position in business.

(4) The President of the Russian Federation is elected to a term of four years. No individual shall be elected as President of the Russian Federation for more than two terms. The procedure for holding elections to the position of President of the Russian Federation is established by law.

(5) The President of the Russian Federation assumes office upon swearing the following oath: "I swear by execution of the powers of the President of the Russian Federation to observe the Constitution and laws of the Russian Federation, to defend its sovereignty, to respect and preserve the rights and freedoms of man and citizen, the rights of the peoples of the Russian Federation and honestly to perform the duties assigned to me." The oath is administered at a joint session of the Chambers of the Supreme Council of the Russian Federation and the Constitutional Court of the Russian Federation. The session is held within 30 days after the election of the Supreme Council of the Russian Federation. The President of the Constitutional Court of the Russian Federation presides at the session.

Article 102

The President of the Russian Federation:

a) directs the activities of the Council of Ministers of the Russian Federation, may chair its sessions, is the Chairman of the Supreme Council of the Russian Federation and the State Council of the Russian Federation; directs the activities of the Federation Business Council and directs general management of other Federal executive organs;

b) represents the Supreme Council of the Russian Federation in the manner established by law for appointment of candidates for the Constitutional Court of the Russian Federation, the SUPREME COURT OF THE RUSSIAN FEDERATION, the Russian Federation Arbitration Court, the Chairman of the Administration of the Russian Federation Central Bank, and the Russian Federation Procurator General;

c) with the consent of the Supreme Council of the Russian Federation appoints the Chairman and members of the Council of Ministers of the Russian Federation, the Russian Federation State Secretary and the Russian Federation State Councilors;

d) appoints Federal Commissioners in the republics and lands, as well as other officials in the Russian Federation executive system;

e) discharges the Chairman and members of the Council of Ministers of the Russian Federation, and other officials whom he appoints;

f) appoints and recalls diplomatic representatives of the Russian Federation, receives the credentials and letters of recall of accredited diplomatic representatives;

g) conducts negotiations and signs international agreements of the Russian Federation, including interstate agreements within the union (commonwealth) of sovereign states;

h) presents annual reports to the Supreme Council of the Russian Federation on the execution of Federal programs, the conduct of domestic and foreign policy of the Russian Federation, gives speeches to the people and to the Supreme Council;

i) with the consent of the Supreme Council of the Russian Federation, calls referenda of the Russian Federation and all-Russian elections;

j) is the Commander in Chief of the Russian Federation armed forces, appoints, with the consent of the Supreme Council of the Russian Federation, and relieves from duty the high command of the armed forces, awards high military ranks, and takes steps to assure state, public and ecological security of the Russian Federation, and the execution of its defense policy;

k) declares states of emergency;

l) resolve questions of citizenship in the Russian Federation in accordance with the law;

m) declares pardons for citizens convicted by courts of the Russian Federation;

n) presents awards of state of the Russian Federation, awards honorable ranks of the Russian Federation and special ranks;

o) performs other duties assigned to him by the Constitution and laws of the Russian Federation.

Article 103

The President of the Russian Federation enjoys immunity and the protection of the law.

Article 104

(1) The President of the Russian Federation, in exercising his duties, publishes orders and decrees, which shall not contradict the Constitution or laws of the Russian Federation and are binding throughout the territory of the Russian Federation.

(2) The President of the Russian Federation may create deliberative bodies, the status of which is determined by Federal law.

Article 105

(1) The President may be relieved of duty in cases of his intentional violation of the Constitution or other laws of the Russian Federation. Impeachment of the President of the Russian Federation is initiated by either Chamber of the Supreme Council of the Russian Federation by vote of 2/3 of its deputies. In this case, the matter is referred to the Constitutional Court of the Russian Federation, which renders its decision as to whether there is basis for relieving the President of his duties. If there is such a

basis, the other Chamber of the Supreme Council of the Russian Federation are empowered to relieve the President of the Russian Federation of his duties by vote of at least 2/3 of its deputies.

(2) Persons relieved of duty as President of the Russian Federation are to be held liable for violations of law.

Article 106

(1) The Vice-President of the Russian Federation is elected in conjunction with the President of the Russian Federation. His candidacy is declared by the candidate for President of the Russian Federation. A vote for a candidate for President of the Russian Federation is a vote for the candidate he has designated for Vice-President of the Russian Federation. A candidate for Vice-President of the Russian Federation must meet the requirements contained in article 108 of this Constitution.

(2) When instructed by the President of the Russian Federation, the Vice-President of the Russian Federation may perform a portion of the duties of President. The Vice-President of the Russian Federation performs the duties of the President of the Russian Federation if the President is temporarily unable to perform his duties. In this case, the powers assumed by the Vice-President of the Russian Federation must be approved by the Supreme Council of the Russian Federation within 3 days.

(3) In case of the death of the President of the Russian Federation; his dismissal; a determination by the Constitutional Court of the Russian Federation that the President of the Russian Federation is unable to perform his duties, or in cases where he is relieved of his duties, the Vice-President of the Russian Federation assumes the office of President of the Russian Federation through the period of the next presidential elections, yet for a period not to exceed six months, during which time elections must be held.

(4) The Vice-President of the Russian Federation is relieved of duty for the same causes and by the came procedure as the President of the Russian Federation.

(5) In case of the death of the Vice-President of the Russian Federation; his dismissal; a determination by the Constitutional Court of the Russian Federation that the Vice President is unable to perform his duties, or in cases where he is relieved of duty and also in case the Vice-President of the Russian Federation assumes the duty of President of the Russian Federation, the President of the Russian Federation appoints the Vice-President of the Russian Federation. He assumes his office after his approval by a majority

of the elected deputies of both Chambers of the Supreme Council of the Russian Federation.

(6) If both the President and Vice-President of the Russian Federation are simultaneously incapable of performing their duties, the office of President of the Russian Federation proceeds through an established order of succession to the President of the Federal Council, the President of the State Duma, the Chairman of the Council of Ministers of the Russian Federation, for a term of up to six months.

CHAPTER XIX. THE FEDERAL EXECUTIVE POWER SYSTEM

Article 107

The Federal executive power system headed by the President of the Russian Federation includes:

a) The Russian Federation State Council;
b) The Russian Federation Security Council;
c) The Russian Federation Council of Ministers.

Article 108

(1) The State Council of the Russian Federation develops recommendations for the President of the Russian Federation on the primary directions of domestic and foreign policy of the Russian Federation, makes suggestions for implementation in cases when legislative initiatives by the President of the Russian Federation to the Supreme Council of the Russian Federation are required, and also supports the interaction of the President of the Russian Federation with the state organs and institutions, the republics and lands, and public associations.

(2) The State Council of the Russian Federation includes *ex officio* the President of the Russian Federation, the Vice-President of the Russian Federation, the Chairman of the Council of Ministers of the Russian Federation, the Secretary of State of the Russian Federation, the State Councilors of the Russian Federation, and certain ministers.

(3) The organization and procedures of the State Council of the Russian Federation are established by Federal law.

Article 109

(1) The Supreme Council of the Russian Federation considers problems of defense, state, economic and ecological security, prevention and dealing with the results of emergency situations, assurance of law and order in society. The Supreme Council of the Russian Federation makes recommendations to the President of the Russian Federation concerning the conduct of policy in these areas and the performance if necessary of legislative initiative in the Supreme Council of the Russian Federation.

(2) The Supreme Council of the Russian Federation includes *ex officio* the Chairman of the Council of Ministers of the Russian Federation, the Directors of Federal departments responsible for defense and security of the Russian Federation, as well as other persons designated by the President of the Russian Federation.

(3) The organization and procedures of operation of the Supreme Council of the Russian Federation are established by Federal law.

Article 110

(1) The Council of Ministers of the Russian Federation is an executive organ that operates under the leadership and authority of the President of the Russian Federation and shall answer to him.

(2) The Council of Ministers of the Russian Federation consists of the Chairman of the Council of Ministers of the Russian Federation, his Deputy Ministers and others outlined by law. The Chairman of the Council of Ministers of the Russian Federation coordinates the activities of the members of the Council of Ministers of the Russian Federation and handles ongoing management of its operations.

(3) The members of the Council of Ministers of the Russian Federation may not function as deputies, members of elected bodies of local government, officials of the state or local governments, may not engage in business activity, nor be members of the administrative bodies of commercial firms, or perform professional duties.

(4) The Council of Ministers of the Russian Federation executes state power of the higher government organs of the Russian Federation and answers to the President of the Russian Federation. In performing its duties, the Council of Ministers of the Russian Federation independently determines the manner by which resolutions and orders are prepared and adopted. These

acts are issued on the basis of and in the execution of the Constitution and other laws of the Russian Federation, together with decrees of the President of the Russian Federation, and are binding over the entire territory of the Russian Federation. The President is authorized to alter or rescind acts of the Council of Ministers of the Russian Federation.

(5) The Council of Ministers of the Russian Federation reports each year on its activity to the Supreme Council of the Russian Federation. Upon request of either Chamber, the Council of Ministers of the Russian Federation or any of its members is obligated to present a report on the subject named in the request, if said subject lies within the scope of his responsibilities.

(6) The status of the Council of Ministers of the Russian Federation and its organs is regulated by Federal Law.

Article 111

(1) Motions of confidence in the Council of Ministers of the Russian Federation shall be voted on by either Chamber of the Supreme Council of the Russian Federation or by no fewer than 100 deputies of the Russian Federation. The question of confidence in the Council of Ministers of the Russian Federation may also be presented to the Council of Ministers of the Russian Federation by the President of the Russian Federation.

(2) The question of confidence in the Council of Ministers of the Russian Federation is considered to be affirmed if one half of the elected deputies of each Chamber vote for a resolution of confidence.

(3) In case of a vote of no confidence in the Council of Ministers of the Russian Federation by the Supreme Council of the Russian Federation, the President of the Russian Federation dissolves the Council of Ministers of the Russian Federation.

Article 112

(1) The Service (administration) of the President of the Russian Federation is a supplementary organ that assists the President of the Russian Federation in the performance of his state duties.

(2) The Service (administration) of the President of the Russian Federation includes advisor, counsel, monitoring, technical and supplementary sections.

(3) The powers, organization and operational procedures of the Service (administration) of the President of the Russian Federation are established by Federal law.

Article 113

(1) Federal powers are exercised in the republics, lands and locally by the Federal territorial services.

(2) The activity of the territorial services of the Federal departments in the republics and lands are coordinated by the Federal Commissioners, designated by the President of the Russian Federation. The composition, location and territorial subordination of the Federal services are determined by the President of the Russian Federation.

(3) The Federal Territorial Services in the republics, lands and locally directly enforce the Federal laws and other acts of the Federal organs in relation to problems related to administration of the Russian Federation. These services likewise endeavor to assure coordinated enforcement of laws and other acts with respect to problems related to the administration of the Russian Federation, republics, lands and self-governing territorial associations. Such services shall not encroach upon the powers of the republics, lands or self-governing territorial associations.

CHAPTER XX. PRIMARY ORGANIZATIONS OF GOVERNMENT OF REPUBLICS AND LANDS

Article 114

(1) The system of governmental organs of the republics and lands is formulated in accordance with the principle of separation of powers established by the present Constitution.

(2) Republican or land governmental organs consist of:
a) the legislative assembly;
b) the executive, elected by the citizens or legislative assembly;
c) the government, headed by the head of the government, responsible to the legislative assembly [Variant: and the President of the Russian Federation];
d) the superior court of the republic or land, as well as local courts.

(3) The republic or land independently determines the form of the organs of the legislative, executive and judicial powers in its own constitution.

(4) Republics and lands may institute local executive services of the republics and lands in their own territory within the limits of their authority.

CHAPTER XXI. LOCAL SELF GOVERNMENT

Article 115

(1) Local self-government is administered by the population through councils, local administrations, local referenda, meetings of citizens, other territorial forms of direct democracy, as well as organs of territorial public self government of the population.

(2) Local self government is administered by territorial associations within the limits of the territorial units into which the republics and lands are divided.

(3) The organization and activity of local self government are regulated by the constitution and laws of the republics and lands.

Article 116

(1) The self government authority of a territorial association includes:
a) the local budget;
b) establishment of local taxes and duties, as specified by the laws of the republic or land;
c) the resolution of economic, communal, social, cultural, ecological and other problems of local significance, as defined by the laws of the republics and lands.

(2) The organs of local self government, within the limits of their authority, act independently of the state government within the Constitution and laws of the Russian Federation, the constitutions and laws of the republics and lands.

Article 117

(1) An organ of local self government (council) is elected by the residents of the territorial units of the republics and lands.

(2) An organ of local self government is a legal entity.

Article 118

(1) Acts of organs of local self government shall not contradict the laws of the Russian Federation, the republics or lands.

(2) The effects of acts adopted by organs of local self government that violate the Constitution or laws of the Russian Federation or the republics or lands may be overturned by the government of the republic or land or the Federal Commissioner of the Russian Federation. The final decision on this question falls to the superior court of the republic or land.

Article 119

Primary territorial collectives of public self government may be created in populated regions, which may create their own associations. Such collectives and their associations have the rights of legal entities.

CHAPTER XXI. LEGAL AUTHORITY

Article 120

(1) Legal authority as the guarantor of civil peace, the rights and freedoms of man and citizen supports law and order in the Russian Federation.

(2) Legal authority in the Russian Federation vests solely to the courts and is exercised in the forms of constitutional, civil, criminal and administrative proceedings.

Article 121

(1) Judges are independent and subject only to the law and conscience. Immunity of judges is guaranteed by law.

(2) Judges, excluding justices of the peace, cannot be removed from office. They are retired when reaching the legally established age.

(3) A judge cannot be relieved of his duties without his consent or only by decision of a court as provided by law. Judges of higher Federal courts are relieved of their duties as provided for in Article [not given - Translator] of this Constitution.

(4) Judges of courts of the republics and lands may be relieved of their duties by the legislative assemblies of the republics and lands.

(5) A judge may not be a deputy, member of a political party, occupy any other paid position or be involved in business. Judges may engage in scientific work or teaching.

Article 122

Citizens of the Russian Federation participate in legal proceedings, which includes fulling obligations to serve as jurors.

Article 123

(1) The court system of the Russian Federation consists of: the Constitutional Court of the Russian Federation, the Supreme Court of the Russian Federation, the Supreme Court of Arbitration of the Russian Federation, other superior Federal courts of the Russian Federation, the courts of the republics and lands, and justices of the peace courts.

(2) The Federal laws and the laws of the republics and lands may establish courts with special jurisdictions. These courts act under general rules for legal proceedings and under the supervision of the Supreme Court of the Russian Federation.

(3) The creation of extraordinary courts and military tribunals is not permitted.

(4) The range of authority, organization and procedures of the Federal courts are determined by Federal laws.

Article 124

No individual shall be deprived of his right to a review of his case in court or by judges, within whose jurisdiction the affair is placed.

Article 125

(1) The Constitutional Court of the Russian Federation, in order to protect the constitutional structure of the Russian Federation, the most important human rights and freedoms, to support the supremacy and direct effect of the Constitution of the Russian Federation in all its territory, considers questions of constitutionality:

a) of international agreements of the Russian Federation, including interstate agreements within the union (commonwealth) of sovereign states prior to their ratification or effective force;

b) the laws of the Russian Federation and other acts of the Supreme Council of the Russian Federation;

c) other legislative acts of the higher governmental organs of the Russian Federation, including acts issued by the President of the Russian Federation and the Council of Ministers of the Russian Federation;

d) laws and other legislative acts of the higher organs of the republics and lands of the Russian Federation;

e) agreements between the Russian Federation and the republics and lands;

f) agreements between the republics and lands;

g) legal practices in the case of individual complaints;

(2) The Constitutional Court of the Russian Federation issues opinions on consistency with the Constitution of the Russian Federation of:

a) actions and decisions of the President of the Russian Federation, the Vice-President of the Russian Federation, and other higher officials of the Russian Federation if, according to the Constitution of the Russian Federation, unconstitutionality of their actions and decisions is grounds for relieving them of their duties;

b) international agreements of the Russian Federation, ratified or taking effect without ratification, including international agreements within the Union (Commonwealth) of Sovereign States.

c) the constitutions of the republics and lands;

(3) The Constitutional Court of the Russian Federation hands down binding interpretations of the Constitution of the Russian Federation.

(4) The Constitutional Court of the Russian Federation renders opinions on the loss by the President of the Russian Federation or Vice-President of the Russian Federation of their ability to perform their duties.

(5) Acts declared unconstitutional by the Constitutional Court of the Russian Federation become invalid as of the day of official publication of the decision of the Constitutional Court of the Russian Federation.

(6) The principles, procedures and conditions under which the Constitutional Court of the Russian Federation operates are determined by Federal law.

Article 126

The Supreme Court of the Russian Federation reviews the judicial actions of the superior courts of the republics and lands in accordance with the processes established by law.

Article 127

(1) Judges shall not have the right to enforce laws that are inconsistent with the Constitution of the Russian Federation.

(2) If a court rules that a proposed law contradicts the Constitution of the Russian Federation, it is bound to cease the proceedings and address the Constitutional Court of the Russian Federation to request a decision on the constitutionality of the law.

Article 128

(1) Court hearings are public. Hearing of cases in closed chambers is permitted only when the court rules that public discussion will reveal state, professional or commercial secrets, or that it is necessary protect personal or family life of the citizens from publicity.

(2) trials in absentia in criminal cases in the lower courts are not permitted.

(3) Court proceedings are conducted on an adversarial basis.

CHAPTER XXIII PROCURATORS AND COMMITTEES OF INQUIRY

Article 129

(1) The procurator is obligated to conduct a criminal investigation in cases of infringement on the rights and freedoms of citizens, the society and the state.

(2) The charges of the state are presented by the procurator in criminal trials in the name of the Russian Federation.

(3) The organization, competence and activity of the procurator are regulated by Federal law.

Article 130

(1) The Committee of Inquiry of the Russian Federation and its organs conduct preliminary investigations in criminal cases.

(2) The organization, jurisdiction and activity of the Committee of Inquiry of the Russian Federation are regulated by Federal laws.

CHAPTER XXV. FINANCES AND BUDGET

Article 131

(1) The state budget system of the Russian Federation includes, as independent parts: the Russian Federation Federal budget, the budgets of the republics and lands, as well as local budgets.
The republics and lands have their own budget systems and enjoy financial independence. The budget policies of the republics and lands are executed in accordance with this Constitution, the constitutions of the republics and lands, and the general principles of the budgetary system established by law.

Article 132

(1) The Russian Federation Federal budget is adopted each year by the Supreme Council of the Russian Federation after presentation by the President of the Russian Federation.

(2) The Supreme Council of the Russian Federation reviews the budget line by line and adopts the Federal budget after receiving the conclusions of the budget committees of the Chambers of the Supreme Council of the Russian Federation and the Russian Federation State Treasury.

(3) The proposed Federal budget is considered by the Chambers of the Supreme Council of the Russian Federation in the manner called for in Article 104 of this Constitution. If agreement is not reached, the Federal budget is adopted at a joint session of the Chambers of the Supreme Council of the Russian Federation by majority vote of the deputies present.

(4) The fiscal year in the Russian Federation begins on 1 January of each calendar year. If the law on the Federal budget has not come into force by the beginning of a fiscal year, then until such a law is in force, expenditures are authorized in accordance with the Federal budget of the previous fiscal

year. In this case, the Supreme Council of the Russian Federation may establish another time period for financing of budgeted expenditures.

(5) In case the Supreme Council of the Russian Federation adopts a Federal budget with an excess of expenditures over income, the sources and methods used to cover the deficit are as provided for by the Federal budget laws.

Article 133

(1) The income of the Federal budget consists of the Federal taxes, duties, payment obligations, income from state property and other Federal income.

(2) The expenditures of the Federal budget include the items of the expended portion of the Federal budget.

(3) The Supreme Council of the Russian Federation has the legal right to establish off-budget dedicated funds and monitor their utilization. The sources of off-budget funds may be both dedicated funds and budgeted expenditures.

Article 134

(1) The President provides the Supreme Council with a line-by-line report on the implementation of the Federal budget within two months after the end of each budget year.

(2) The Supreme Council is obligated to consider the report within 3 months after its presentation based on the conclusions of the budget committees of the Supreme Council of the Russian Federation and the State Treasury.

(3)The report presented on the implementation of the Federal budget is published.

Article 135

The Central Bank of the Russian Federation is subordinate to the Supreme Council of the Russian Federation, and independent from the executive organs.

Article 136

(1) The State Treasury of the Russian Federation is subordinate to the Supreme Council of the Russian Federation and independent of other state organs.

(3) The powers, organization and procedures of the State Treasury of the Russian Federation are established by Federal law.

CHAPTER XXVI. DEFENSE AND SECURITY

Article 137

(1) The Russian Federation may create armed forces for the defense of its state sovereignty and territorial integrity.

(2) The armed forces include regular professional and draft units as well as a Federal guard.

(3) The military doctrine, structure and organization of the Russian Federation armed forces and other composite elements of the defense policy are determined by law.

(4) In accordance with Article 10 of this Constitution, the Russian Federation may conclude defensive unions with other states, create, on the basis of treaties, combined armed forces, including strategic forces and combined Commands.

Article 138

(1) The protection of public law and order is the responsibility of the Federal organs of internal affairs, the Federal and local police.

Article 139

(1) The use of the armed forces, security services, internal affairs organs and police for the purpose of overthrowing the constitutional order, obstructing or limiting the activity of the higher organs of state authority, illegal limitation of constitutional rights and freedoms of citizens is a felony.

(2) A declaration by the Supreme Council of the Russian Federation that the armed forces, security services or militia have been used illegally demands immediate parliamentary investigation.

Article 140

The duties of ministers responsible for problems of defense and security in the Council of Ministers of the Russian Federation shall be fulfilled by civilians.

CHAPTER XXIV. THE GOVERNMENT SERVICE

Article 141

(1) Persons occupying civilian positions in government organs and institutions are in government service. Government service personnel bear the responsibility for failure to enforce the laws and other acts of the Russian Federation or for unreliable enforcement. Political party organizations shall not be established in the civil service system.

(2) Citizens of the Russian Federation have equal access to government service. The requirements for candidates for government service positions are determined solely by the nature of the duties involved.

(3) The procedure for entering government service, its conduct, the qualifications, duties and special ranks, release from duty, and other questions of government service are regulated by the Federal laws.

CHAPTER XXVII. STATES OF EMERGENCY

Article 142

(1) A state of emergency refers to a special legal mode of action of the organs of the government, enterprises, institutions and organizations, that respects the rights and freedoms of the citizens and the rights of legal entities called for by this Constitution and Federal laws to be exercised, yet also placing additional obligations upon them.

(2) The purpose of declaration of an state of emergency is to achieve as rapidly as possible a return to the normal conditions of society.

(3) A state of emergency is a temporary measure and may be declared solely in the interests of society, the security of the citizens and the defense of the democratic constitutional structure.

(4) A state of emergency is declared for the entire territory of the Russian Federation or for individual regions.

(5) The state of emergency is regulated by this Constitution and the Federal laws.

Article 143

(1) A state of emergency may be declared only under conditions such that the factors serving as the basis for declaration of the emergency condition represent a real, extreme and inevitable threat to the safety of the citizens or constitution order, elimination of which is impossible without the use of extreme measures.

(2) The basis for declaration of an emergency may be:

a) attempts to change the constitutional order by force, massive disorders accompanied by force, ethnic conflict, blockades of individual locations, threats to the life and safety of the citizens or normal activity of government institutions;

b) natural calamities, epidemics, disasters and catastrophes, posing an immediate threat to the life and health of the population and requiring emergency rescue and reclamation operations.

Article 144

In situations requiring emergency measures to save the population, a state of emergency may be declared immediately and without advance notification.

Article 145

(1) A state of emergency involving the entire territory of the Russian Federation or individual locations is declared by decree of the President of the Russian Federation with immediate notification of the Russian Federation Supreme Council.

(2) If a decree of a state of emergency is published during a working session of the Supreme Council of the Russian Federation, the Supreme Council of the Russian Federation must consider it within 24 hours. In other cases, the Supreme Council of the Russian Federation must consider the decree within 72 hours from the moment it is published.

(3) If the Supreme Council of the Russian Federation does not confirm the decision of the President of the Russian Federation, the decree of the state of emergency becomes invalid.

Article 146

(1) If a state of emergency is declared only in the territory of one republic (or land) of the Russian Federation, preliminary notification of the republic (land) is required.

(2) The declaration of a state of emergency without the agreement of the republic (or land) is permitted only in order to quell massive disorders accompanied by force.

(3) If the situation serving as the basis for declaration of the state of emergency involves the territory of only one republic (or land) of the Russian Federation, the state of emergency in this republic (or land) may be declared by the republic or land, with notification of the President and Supreme Council of the Russian Federation and in observance of the requirements of this Constitution and Federal law.

(4) Declaration of a state of emergency for the reasons indicated in item b) of part (2) of Article 150 of this Constitution is permitted only with the agreement of the republic or land involved if its governmental organs continue normal operation.

Article 147

A state of emergency cannot be declared for more than 30 days over the entire territory of the Russian Federation or more than sixty days for a portion of the territory of the Russian Federation. After this time has passed, the state of emergency is terminated, unless the Supreme Council extends the term.

The Supreme Council can extend a state of emergency for periods of no more than 30 additional days.

Article 148

(1) The population shall be warned in advance of the imposition, continuation or termination of a state of emergency by all available means.

(2) Acts declaring, continuing or terminating a state of emergency must be published.

Article 149

(1) The Constitution, elections laws of the Russian Federation, and laws concerning judicial processes may not be amended during a state of emergency, nor may referenda or elections of state organs or officials be held.

(2) The powers and activity of the Supreme Council of the Russian Federation and the courts of the Russian Federation may not be interrupted or limited during a state of emergency.

Article 150

(1) The President of the Russian Federation may introduce temporary limitations on the rights and freedoms of citizens during a state of emergency. These limitations must be directly declared in the text of the decree of the emergency. The rights and freedoms described in Articles 22, 23(2), 28, 29, 34, 36, 41, 45, 47, 49 and 50 in the draft of 16/09/91 of this Constitution cannot be limited.

(2) The President of the Russian Federation immediately informs all states participating in international agreements, establishing the freedoms and rights which have been limited, of the limitations, their causes, and their termination.

(3) Judicial proceedings relating to capital crimes cannot be held during a state of emergency and for 30 days after termination of the state of emergency.

Article 151

Measures taken during a state of emergency:

a) must be limited to those required by the seriousness of the situation;

b) may not place any limitations on or involve any changes in the rights and privileges of the governmental organs and administrations, the legal status of public organizations, or the rights and freedoms of man in other areas, not involved in the state of emergency;

c) must not involve any discrimination against individuals or groups of the population on the basis of race, skin color, nationality, sex, language, religion, property position or social origin.

SECTION VI. CONCLUDING STATEMENTS

CHAPTER XXVIII. CAPITAL AND STATE SYMBOLS OF THE RUSSIAN FEDERATION

Article 152

(1) The Capital of the Russian Federation is the city of Moscow.

(2) The city of Moscow and the surrounding area (oblast') form the capital area, the status of which is determined by Federal law.

Article 153

(1) The State Flag of the Russian Federation is a banner of three equal-sized horizontal white, azure and red bands.

(2) The description of the State Coat of Arms of the Russian Federation is determined by Federal law.

(3) The State Anthem of the Russian Federation is the "Patriotic Song" of M Glinka as arranged by A. Petrov. The text of the State Anthem of the Russian Federation is defined by Federal law.

CHAPTER XXIX. LEGAL PERIOD WHERE THE CONSTITUTION OF THE RUSSIAN FEDERATION BECOMES LAW

Article 154

(1) This Constitution will become law the day after the official publication of the results of a referendum of the RSFSR (All-Russian National Election) on the Constitution of the Russian Federation.

(2) The official day this Constitution of the Russian Federation becomes law will be a state holiday.

(3) The individual parts of this Constitution indicated in the section on "Transitional Items" will become law at the times designated in those items.

Article 155

On the day the Constitution of the Russian Federation becomes law, the Constitution (Primary Law) of the RSFSR of 1978 and its subsequent amendments and additions shall become null and void.

CHAPTER XXX. PROCEDURE FOR AMENDMENT OF THE CONSTITUTION OF THE RUSSIAN FEDERATION

Article 156

Proposed amendments of the Constitution of the Russian Federation may be submitted:

a) by at least one fifth of the elected deputies of either Chamber of the Supreme Council of the Russian Federation;

b) by the legislative assembly of a republic or land.

Article 157

(1) The Supreme Council of the Russian Federation has the right to adopt a law on amendment of the Constitution of the Russian Federation no earlier than one half year after the proposed amendment is submitted. The draft of the law must be approved by the Committee on Constitutional Reform of the Supreme Council of the Russian Federation and approved by two thirds of the elected deputies of each of the Chambers of the Supreme Council of the Russian Federation.

(2) If within one year after submission of a proposed amendment to the Constitution of the Russian Federation the Supreme Council of the Russian Federation does not approve the corresponding law, the proposed amendment is considered rejected and cannot be resubmitted during the following year.

TRANSITIONAL PROVISIONS

I. LEGISLATION OF THE RUSSIAN FEDERATION

Section 1.

1. The laws to which reference is made in the Constitution of the Russian Federation must be adopted during the year after it becomes law. If such laws are in effect when the Constitution of the Russian Federation becomes law, they shall remain in effect until revised, insofar as they do not violate this Constitution.

2. The Federal, republic and local enforceable enactments, to which no reference is made in the Constitution of the Russian Federation, must be reconciled with the Constitution within a three year period following the date on which the Constitution of the Russian Federation becomes law. Such enactments shall continue to be legally binding through this date insofar as they do not violate the Constitution of the Russian Federation or Federal laws.

3. Laws and other enforceable enactments of the USSR are binding on the territory of the Russian Federation insofar as they do not violate this Constitution nor the international agreements to which the Russian Federation is a party.

4. The provisions outlined in (3) of this section also apply to international agreements to which the USSR is a party. However, the provisions of international agreements to which the USSR is a party that violate the Constitution of the Russian Federation shall be nullified in the manner provided for in procedures for amendment or renunciation of international agreements to which the Russian Federation is a party. Prior to said nullification the international agreements to which the USSR is a party shall remain in force for the Russian Federation, if the Russian Federation is the successor to the USSR with respect to those agreements.

II. THE RIGHTS, FREEDOMS AND OBLIGATIONS OF MAN AND CITIZEN

Section 2.

1. Citizenship in the Russian Federation is indivisible. Each citizen of the Russian Federation retains citizenship in the USSR.

2. All citizens of the USSR permanently residing on the territory of the Russian Federation on the day the Constitution of the Russian Federation becomes law are legally citizens of the Russian Federation, if said citizens do not provide notification in writing of their desire to reject citizenship in the Russian Federation to a local internal affairs organ within a one year period.

3. Individuals born or having at least one parent born within the territory of the Russian Federation have the legal option of adopting citizenship in the Russian Federation within a period of one year after the Constitution of the Russian Federation becomes law in accordance with the procedure established by Federal law.

4. Citizenship in the Russian Federation may be adopted in accordance with the procedure established by law within one year after the Constitution of the Russian Federation becomes law.

Section 3.

A Federal law shall be adopted to regulate the transition to an orderly implementation of the right to free selection of a place of residence within one year after the Constitution of the Russian Federation becomes law. This transition shall be completed within a period of 10 years after the law goes into effect.

Section 4.

1. The "nationality" column shall be deleted from identification documents (passports, birth certificates, etc.), as it is of no significance in terms of an individual's legal status.

2. Documents to be completed upon employment and in other cases unrelated to a census of the population shall not include questions concerning nationality, party membership, location in occupied territory during the

Great Patriotic War or other data relating to the future activity of the individual. Exceptions will be established by Federal law.

3. Requests that employees answer such questions, except in cases established by law, are illegal and represent a disciplinary offense. A corresponding Federal law shall to be adopted within 6 months after the Constitution of the Russian Federation becomes law.

III. REGULATION OF ECONOMIC RELATIONS

Section 5.

Government regulation of economic activity within the limits and in accordance with the procedures established by Federal law is permitted during the period of transition to a market economy, in order to assure social and economic stability.

Section 6.

The credit and monetary system in effect in the Russian Federation on the day this Constitution becomes law shall remain in effect pending regulation of credit and monetary relationships among the states comprising the Union of Soviet Socialist Republics and adoption of a special Federal law.

Section 7.

Intergovernmental organs and institutions are financed in accordance with the international agreements of the Russian Federation, including intergovernmental agreements within the union (commonwealth) of sovereign states.

IV. THE FEDERATIVE STRUCTURE

Section 8

1. The republics within the RSFSR on the day this Constitution becomes law acquire by right the status of republics of the Russian Federation, as provided for in Section IV of the Constitution of the Russian Federation. Autonomous oblasts and autonomous okrugs shall have the right to retain their status of national autonomy for a period of 10 years after formation of the republics and lands.

2. Krays, oblasts, autonomous oblasts, and autonomous okrugs are unified and comprise lands which are direct constituent elements of the Russian Federation in the manner provided for by Federal law. In exceptional cases a land may be formed in the territory of a single kray or oblast.

3. The Federal law on the conditions and manner of formation of lands of the Russian Federation must be adopted within 1 year after this Constitution becomes law. Lands must be formed no later than 31 December 1993. Pending formation of lands, the status of krays and oblasts is regulated by the law for administration of a kray or oblast. The laws of the RSFSR concerning autonomous oblasts and okrugs are applied, insofar as they do not violate this Constitution.

V. THE SYSTEM OF STATE POWER

Section 9-A [VARIANT A]

When this Constitution of the Russian Federation becomes law the people's deputies of the RSFSR shall become the deputies of the Supreme Council of the Russian Federation. The people's deputies of the RSFSR elected in territorial elective districts will form the State Duma. The people's deputies of the RSFSR elected in national-territorial elective districts will form the Federal Council. During the current session of the Supreme Council of the Russian Federation, the Chambers shall have the right to adopt resolutions by majority vote of the deputies present. The sessions of the Chambers are valid if at least one half the deputies of the Federal Council and at least one third of the deputies of the State Duma are present.

Section 9-B [VARIANT B]

When this Constitution of the Russian Federation becomes law, all people's deputies of the RSFSR shall become deputies of the Russian Federation. The Supreme Soviet of the RSFSR shall be converted to the Supreme Council of the Russian Federation. Deputies of the Russian Federation who are not deputies of the Supreme Council of the Russian Federation have the same rights, obligations and guarantees as deputies of the Supreme Council of the Russian Federation, including the right to participate in the organs of the Supreme Council of the Russian Federation on a permanent basis. At sessions of the Chambers, the deputies of the Russian Federation have the right of deliberative vote. All deputies of the Russian Federation retain their mandates until their term of office expires. Congresses of Russian Federation deputies will not be held.

Section 9-C [VARIANT C]

Elections for the Supreme Council of the Russian Federation shall be held upon completion of the reform of the Federal structure, no later than 1994.

Section 9-D [VARIANT D]

1. When this Constitution of the Russian Federation becomes law, all people's deputies of the RSFSR shall become deputies of the Russian Federation. The Supreme Soviet of the RSFSR will be converted to the Supreme Council of the Russian Federation. The deputies of the Russian Federation who are not deputies of the Supreme Council of the Russian Federation have the same rights, obligations and guarantees as do deputies of the Supreme Council of the Russian Federation, including the right to participate in the work of organs of the Supreme Council of the Russian Federation on a permanent basis. Deputies of the Russian Federation have the right of deliberative vote at sessions of the Chambers. All deputies of the Russian Federation retain their mandates until their term of office expires.

2. The Soviet of Nationalities shall be converted to a Federal Council, consisting of 150 deputies. The members of the Federal Council may become deputies elected from national-territorial election districts and regional deputies of groups of the corresponding national-territorial formations, krays, oblasts, the cities of the Moscow and St. Petersburg, delegated in the Federal Council. The existing standards for representation are retained. In cases when the regional groups of deputies elected from national-territorial districts cannot elect a sufficient number of members of the Federal Council from among themselves, they retain the right to delegate to the Federal Council deputies elected from the national-territorial districts of another region, taking on themselves the obligation to represent in the Federal Council the interests of the region assigned to them.

3. The Republic Soviet is converted to the State Duma, consisting of 300 deputies. Deputies elected in territorial districts may become members of the State Duma. One hundred fifty members of the State Duma consist groups of deputies of the corresponding national-territorial formations, krays and oblasts, and the cities of Moscow and St. Petersburg. The existing norms for representation are preserved. Another 150 members of the State Duma are consist of political factions and other associations created for this purpose in accordance with quotas corresponding to the membership of these registered factions and groups.

4. Subsequent rotating elections of both Chambers of the Supreme Council of the Russian Federation are held in accordance with the standards presented in parts 2 and 3 of this Section.

5. The RSFSR Congress of People's Deputies shall be converted into the Congress of Deputies of the Russian Federation. It shall approve the members of the Supreme Council of the Russian Federation, delegated by groups of deputies and retains its authority through March of 1995. Congresses of deputies of the Russian Federation are routinely held once per year, extraordinary sessions are held in accordance with resolutions of the Supreme Council of the Russian Federation or on demand by 350 deputies. The congress of deputies of the Russian Federation may cede a portion of its authority to the Supreme Council of the Russian Federation.

Section 10

In case of early departure of a deputy of the State Duma during the first session of the Supreme Council of the Russian Federation, election of a new deputy for the remaining portion of the term will not be held; his electoral district will be represented by a deputy from one of the neighboring districts. A resolution to this effect will be adopted by the State Duma.

Section 11

1. Pending adoption of the federal laws regulating the organization and activity of the courts, procurators and investigative organs in accordance with this Constitution, each of these organs in existence on the day the Constitution of the Russian Federation becomes law will continue to operate.

2. Judges of all courts of the Russian Federation, holding their positions on the day the Constitution of the Russian Federation becomes law, retain their authority until their terms expire.

3. The authority of the Procurator General of the RSFSR, provided for by the law of the USSR on procurators, is to be exercised by the Procurator General of the Russian Federation until a new Federal law is adopted.

Section 12

The system of executive governmental organs must be converted by Federal law to the satisfy the requirements of this Constitution within 6 months after it becomes law.

APPENDIX 1

EXPLANATORY NOTES ON THE DRAFT CONSTITUTION OF THE RUSSIAN FEDERATION

1.

THE NEW CONSTITUTION FOR THE RUSSIAN FEDERATION FOUNDING PRINCIPLES

At this critical moment in Russian history we have undertaken a massive constitutional reform. A year ago the draft of the new Constitution of the Russian Federation was born in the depths of the Russian parliament; its basic provisions are familiar to you, since its concepts have been preserved. Some believe that the Constitution forms nascent relationships and institutions. But the history of World civilization knows other examples, in which a Fundamental Law, based on reason and logic, has given birth to a transition to a new structure of life, thereby lending it stability. The new Russian Constitution shall make it possible to follow a constitutional path to avoid the collapse of the government and society, and lay down a solid foundation for the transformations to come.

The new Constitution will make it possible to consolidate the sovereignty of Russia, to give priority to the rights and freedoms of man and citizen, to maintain the democratic nature of government, law and order, to create a progressive governmental apparatus at the center and in the provinces, and to achieve a significant social and economic transformation for the common good.

The Draft Constitution creates guarantees of rights against totalitarianism, provides scope for freedom of choice, honest enterprise and initiative. Henceforth there shall be no official state ideology standing above man. For the first time in the history of Russia, humanistic ideas, based on the inalienability and stability of the rights and freedoms of man and citizen, have been set in place as the foundation of the state. This makes this draft radically different from the declarative provisions of previous constitutions of the RSFSR.

The Constitution shall become a legal document in the strict legal sense, the basis of all legislation, the legal basis of governmental and public life. The text is deideologized, containing no directions as to the nature of the social structure. Determination of this structure is not the task of the Constitution; it is a political task, to be undertaken in the course of natural political, parliamentary life.

It would be possible to create the new structure "as we go", intuitively and in parts. But we wish to proceed otherwise, setting forth in the new Constitution a systematic vision of the state structure, without which both continuing legislation and political practice are doomed.

We feel today quite clearly the demand to establish constitutional balance between the Federation and its parts; between the individual branches of government. The Constitution creates this balance, installing a clear system of separation of powers, both vertically and horizontally. The presence of sufficient mutual checks and balances will give stability to the proposed system, which will arise in the Russian Federation after completion of the reform of the governmental structure.

The Constitution calls for replacement of the current model of relationships: from rigid control of society by the totalitarian government to an effective social contract between the individual, society and government. Man, his rights and freedoms are affirmed as the highest value; society (the self-organized people) is affirmed as the bearer of sovereignty and the sole source of state power; the government is affirmed as the agent of the individual and society, authorized to perform only those tasks assigned to it by the Constitution.

The Constitution has a clear architecture. The logic of construction of the draft is defined by the concept of the social contract: principles of the structure (section I); man (section II); society (section III); the state (vertically -- section IV; horizontally -- section V).

The Constitution is founded on the principles of the social state, the social market economy, and defines the constitutional obligations of the state in the social sphere. The relationship of social partners is affirmed between the citizen and the state, the consumer and the producer, the worker and the employer. The Russian Federation creates the necessary guarantees for such relationships.

The task at hand is not an easy one: not only to adopt the highest law of the Russian Federation, but also to implant the very spirit of constitutionalism, respect for rights and the law, in the daily life of Russia. The new Constitution carries a significant educational load. With the present disorientation of mass consciousness, the changing of fundamental concepts, it sets forth a clear, understandable and firm system of rights and legal landmarks: the immutable PRINCIPLES OF A DEMOCRATIC CONSTITUTIONAL STRUCTURE.

Many of these principles were embodied by the writers in the Declaration of State Sovereignty of the RSFSR. The declaration was a promise; the new Constitution is its fulfillment.

These principles were perceived; it was no accident that many Russians spoke of the new constitutions during the hard days of the August Putsch.

Soviet Russia has known four Constitutions over the past 73 years. The train of corrections between 1988-1991 has actually created a fifth Constitution. The new Constitution will be the sixth Fundamental Law; there have already been seven such laws for Russia in the twentieth century. Yet the promise for further improvements in the structure of life is based on firm constitutional principles, tested by mankind, in the new Constitution. This provides some hope for flexibility, viability and, at the same time, stability of the Russian Constitution.

The adoption of the new Constitution will signify that the Russian Federation has taken its place in the world community as a full-fledged, peace-loving member. The draft provisions reflect the experience of World civilization, general human values, and the heritage of democratic trends in the development of Russian social thought. The Draft Constitution makes a valid contribution to constitutional thought.

The provisions of the draft leave open the possibility of the creation of a union (commonwealth) of sovereign states on the basis of an agreement with those republics that remain in the USSR, as well as with other states.

Attitudes toward the new Draft Constitution have changed over the past year and even over the past few months. It no longer shocks or infuriates, for life itself has confirmed the validity of the ideas embodied in the draft. Some such ideas have already come to life. Many of the provisions (on economic relations, the President, the Constitutional Court and others) have been included in the Constitution of the RSFSR. The corresponding section of the draft was based on the Declaration of Human Rights and Freedoms adopted by the last (extraordinary) Congress of People's Deputies of the USSR.

2.
RIGHTS AND FREEDOMS

In contrast to the Constitution presently in force, which presupposes the antihuman thesis of the "class nature" of rights and freedoms and their subordination to the goals of the state, the understanding of rights, freedoms and obligations of man and citizen underlying the proposed draft is based on a fundamentally different philosophy of natural rights, generally recognized in all civilized nations. The draft is founded on the principle that the rights and freedoms of man vest to him from birth, represent the highest value and have priority over the goals and rights of the government. The main obligation of the state is to observe human rights.

The provisions of the section on the human rights correspond as closely as possible to the Universal Declaration of Human Rights, international pacts and other agreements on the human rights.

The list of established rights and freedoms has itself been considerably expanded. In particular, the right to life; a ban on torture; the right to uninhibited travel to and from the Russian Federation; the right to freely determine one's national allegiance; the right to create political parties; the right to economic freedom and property; the freedom to form labor agreements, etc. are recognized for the first time.

The draft specifically outlines the rights and freedoms affirmed and guaranteed by the state. This is one of its advantages, since many civil rights are incorporated as guarantees. Provisions are included for: legal defense of rights; the presumption of innocence; a court order as the only basis for arrest and other forms of detention; protection from the obligation to testify against oneself, one's spouse and close relatives, etc.

We note particularly the Commissioner on Human Rights, who is the supreme and independent defender of rights with a broad range of rights and powers; the Commissioner on Human Rights answers only to parliament.

Radical innovations are also contained in the chapter on obligations where, in particular, we find: liability for executing a manifestly illegal order; the possibility for performing alternative civil service en lieu of military service, etc.

3. CIVIL SOCIETY

One of the remarkable features of the draft is the special section on "Civil Society."

This section did not appear by accident. It was dictated by the logic behind the design of the Fundamental Law: the progression from the specific and individual (status of the individual) to the legal and general (structure and legal status of the state). Civil society represents the important link between the individual and the state, the social sphere within which most of the rights and freedoms of man are exercised.

A civil society, as is evident from the draft of the new Constitution, includes economic relationships and institutions (property, labor, enterprise); the organization and activity of public associations, political parties, labor unions, creative associations, religious groups, etc.; a sphere of education, science and culture; the family -- the primary natural basis of human society -- and a system of mass media.

The structure of a civil society is established to satisfy the many demands of individuals that largely spring from the bottom up, not from the top down on orders from the state. The elements that comprise a civil society (individuals, collectives) are legally independent of one other, and interact as free and equal partners. A civil society "meshes" the horizontal cooperative connections, which in principle do not have "director (command) -- subordinate" relationships.

A civil society exists with another, equally obvious, reality -- the state. The state integrates all of civil society and has a significant influence on it.

The guiding principles employed in this process include:
a) all that is not specifically proscribed is allowed;
b) the supreme obligation of the state is to serve the interests of the individual and society.

4. THE FEDERATIVE STRUCTURE (PRINCIPLES OF THE CONSTITUTIONAL FEDERATION)

The Constitution transforms Russia into a truly federative state, providing harmony to the entire system of intragovernmental relations. This primarily results from a clear division of powers between the Russian

Federation as a whole and its constituent elements. The fully integrated Federation is strong due to its strong constituent elements. A barrier is set up on the path to chaos and disintegration, wars of laws and jurisdictions, which exact a tremendous price from the multinational people and economy of the Russian Federation.

In formulating this section of the draft, we proceeded from the indisputable affirmation that the Russian Federation is a "sovereign state, created by the peoples historically united in it" (Resolution 3 of the Congress of People's Deputies of the RSFSR of 5th April 1991, Article 1 of the Constitution of the RSFSR). It follows that this state is politically and legally constructed; it exists in actuality and its constituent peoples are already united within it.

To inquire whether it is necessary to once again begin the process of uniting the peoples, to once more proceed with the formation of the Russian Federation (by signing a treaty or by some other means) implies a rejection of reality, the facts and the law.

The primary origins of national-state structures, the distribution of jurisdictions, etc. clearly require legal regulation. However, it is not at all clear why some would like to select as the form of this regulation an act as unclear in its structure and procedure of implementation as a Federation Treaty.

This is not the only element that casts doubt on the notion of a Federation Treaty. One question remains unanswered: who would sign such a treaty? The entities of the Federation, on the one hand, and the Federation as a whole, on the other? But the higher organs of the legislative and executive branches of the Federation represent the peoples and all entities of the same Federation. Or should the entities of the Federation sign the treaty only with each other? But what, specifically, is at this moment an entity of the Federation? According to the spirit and letter of the existing Constitution -- only the republics making up the Federation. No oblasts and krays are as yet included in the Federation. But with this situation, any movement in the direction of concluding a FT is simply absurd. The oblasts and krays (according to the draft Constitution of the Russian Federation -- groups of oblasts and krays are lands) are to be full entities of the Federation and are to have the same identical constitutional and legal status as do the republics. Resolution 3 of the Congress of People's Deputies of the RSFSR calls for granting of this status to krays and oblasts.

The claim that the treaty process can somehow make the Federation more legitimate, more acceptable for the people united within it by giving them the opportunity to express the will of the entities of the Federation in full measure, allowing them to construct state power "from the bottom up" and with their active participation on the scale of the whole Russian state, is also used to argue in favor of concluding a FT. This argument likewise fails from both the legal and legislative viewpoints.

Regardless of the type of treaty we consider, in the final analysis it reduces to a willing or unwilling recognition of the statehood of the Russian Federation, which exists, has already been formed and functions at present. An FT proposes somehow to construct it afresh. The inconsistency of such a damaging, threatening position, which essentially would lead to the destruction of the RSFSR as a single, integrated state, was mentioned above. We should note here that the world experience of constitutionalism has never included and does not yet include examples of such strange treaties. Furthermore, the process of concluding such a treaty among more than 70 entities would be infinitely difficult and unpromising.

The proponents of the Federation Treaty clearly oppose Resolution 3 of the Congress of People's Deputies of the RSFSR and the draft Constitution of the Russian Federation (particularly its section on the "Federative Structure") on artificial grounds. A comparison of the text of this Resolution to the draft Constitution clearly demonstrates a great commonality between these two documents. The Russian Federation is acknowledged to be a unified, sovereign state in both documents. The laws adopted by the entities of the Federation within the limits of their sovereignty are recognized to be legally binding within their territory; the krays and oblasts are assumed to be units, destined to become full subjects of the Federation. This very important fact does not vitiate the legal status of the republics (although there are those who attempt to paint a different picture).

In other words, the corresponding problems are solved effectively and in an acceptable manner in the draft Constitution.

Section IV of the draft makes significant changes to the territorial organization of Russia. Today, as we know, Russia is a federation in name only. All the territory of the Russian Federation, as we propose to name our state, emphasizing its federative nature, will consist of the territories of its subjects -- the republics and lands, which will have identical constitutional and legal status. It is proposed that the present krays, oblasts, autonomous oblasts, and autonomous okrugs unify on the basis of economic, economic-geographic and other naturally existing connections and form lands, which will become powerful territorial associations. Only in exceptional cases can the status of a land be given to a single presently existing kray or oblast.

The draft Constitution defines the sphere of authority of the Federal government and, separately, the sphere of authority of the Federation and its subjects. Beyond these limits each republic or land exercises its authority independently, and the Federal organs have no right to interfere in these areas.

The means are provided for signing treaties and agreements between individual republics, and lands and with the Federation as a whole. Specifically, the authority of the Federation and its subjects may be redistributed by such agreements, thereby providing the system with the necessary flexibility.

The relevant republic or land is authorized to determine the territorial structure of independent associations and, therefore, to establish such associations and regulate their status.

This section of the draft also answers the question of official languages. In addition to the Russian language, which is used in all government organs and institutions, each republic and land may establish other official languages to be used in its governmental organs and institutions.

5.
GOVERNMENT OF LAWS

The draft is based on contemporary constitutional thought, as well as the experience of Russian constitutionalism of the early 20th century.

The events of this period provided the impetus for the movement toward a government of laws in Russia. As we know, many government acts of 1905-1906 established legislation of a constitutional nature. The Manifesto of 17 October 1905 created the State Duma with legislative functions. Russia established a parliament for the first time. It is no accident that one of the Chambers of the new Supreme Council of the Russian Federation is to be named the State Duma. The Manifesto introduced a number of liberal changes, contained provisions emphasizing the desire for a legal structure, proclaimed civil rights and freedoms based on the inviolability of the individual, as well as freedom of conscience, speech, assembly and association.

The provisions of the Manifesto served as the basis for the adoption on 23 April 1906 of the Fundamental Laws, which were the first Russian

Constitution. The theoreticians of the new government in Russia had no doubt that it existed solely due to the separation of powers, which is possible only in a constitutional government.

The draft of the new Constitution, in the section on the state power system of the Russian Federation, sets forth the relationship among the legislative, executive and judicial branches, such that the idea of separation of powers is implemented in fact. In our opinion, this has been successfully achieved. The implementation of a true constitutional order for Russia is a necessary prerequisite for the rule of law.

One of the most important conditions for the implementation of a true constitutional state is the rule of law. In a constitutional state, the government yields to law, not the law to government.

Article 6 of the draft affirms the principle of separation of powers, with all branches of the government acting independently, in balance and in concert. The draft provides for no extragovernmental organs.

The draft Constitution is depoliticized. Obviously, the law must be valid and in force quite independently of the political trends present in the country and government. The law, by its very nature, stands above political passions and it is a perversion to subject it to such passions. The existence of the state of law is also clearly reflected in the draft Constitution.

6.
SYSTEM OF GOVERNMENTAL POWER

The draft suggests a system combining a strong elected Federal parliament, a Supreme Council of the Russian Federation, elected by the people; a president -- the head of the government and the executive branch, with sufficient authority, also elected by the people and a strong and independent judicial branch.

A model close to a presidential republic was selected, yet this model incorporated a number of modifications to allow for the uniqueness of the Russian past and Russian reality.

The president leads the government which he appoints. The government is simultaneously supervised by the parliament.

The idea of integrating the system of executive power -- the president and the government of the entire Russian Federation, the governments of the republics and lands, local administrations acting in cooperation and strictly within the limits of their authority -- is adopted.

The separation of powers implies not only their distribution and demonopolization, but also a mutual balance, a system of mutual checks and balances, the achievement of civil agreement on the basis of the principle of a pluralistic democracy and the rule of law. Under such conditions, no single branch can overpower another branch (subordinate or rise above that branch) and all branches are forced to operate under conditions of interdependence.

Given the destabilization and crisis that exist today, it is important to create a strong executive branch that is capable of action. But this cannot be an absolute goal. It is no less important to elevate the legislator and the judge to the same level. Otherwise the parliament becomes a fifth wheel. Considering the ancient traditions of Russia, it is no less important to create a genuine parliamentary tradition that places the executive under the rule of law. It is also important to remember the judicial branch.

7. THE NEW PARLIAMENT

The Supreme Council of the Russian Federation, according to the draft Constitution, is the highest organ of representative government and the only legislative branch in the Russian Federation.

This is a democratic parliament that represents the entire population of the Russian Federation. It is formed on the basis of universal and free suffrage. However, it also reflects the federative structure of the Russian Federation: the deputies of one Chamber are elected in direct proportion to the population of their representative districts, while the deputies of the other Chamber are elected in accordance with quotas intended to balance the representation of the republics and lands independent of their respective populations.

The Supreme Council of the Russian Federation is the most important element in the system of separation of powers. Having the exclusive right to issue and amend laws, it determines the framework within which the executive and judicial branches operate. Its strongest influence on the executive branch is through the approval and control of the budget, its role in the appointment and transfer of members of the government and other officials and its supervisory functions (parliamentary investigations, hearings, etc.)

The Supreme Council is a standing organ. This is achieved by its efficient organization (the great majority of its work is carried out in the Chambers, commissions and committees and their specialization), as well as the efficient staffing and professional training level of the deputies.

The Supreme Council is a politically stable institution as stipulated by the draft Constitution. This is guaranteed by the fact that it is a permanently-standing organ that convenes by law within a precisely defined period following elections, may be dissolved solely by its own resolution and has the authority to override a presidential veto of adopted laws.

The Supreme Council has the necessary legal tools to inhibit anticonstitutional and illegal actions regardless of their origin. In specific cases it may remove from office not only any individual official, but even the President himself. The Supreme Council also controls the declaration and termination of states of emergency, may demand submission of any information, etc.

The draft Constitution does not provide for a position of President of the Supreme Council of the Russian Federation or the creation of a Presidium of the Supreme Council of the Russian Federation. The Chambers of the Supreme Council of the Russian Federation will operate independently under the leadership of a Chairman elected in each Chamber; at Joint Sessions of the Chambers, which are held only in certain cases and cannot be called for the purpose of debating or adopting laws, the Chairmen of the Chambers will preside in turn.

According to the draft Constitution the authority of the Presidium of the Supreme Soviet is to be distributed among the Chambers. With the Chambers of the Supreme Council convened on a standing basis, there is no need for such an organ as a Presidium, which actually legislated between sessions. It is necessary to reject the idea of replacing the directly elected legislative organs with other organs, to which the Supreme Council might "subcontract" its normal activity.

It is also important to consider the fact that the expanded independence of the Chambers, whereby each Chamber acquires its own unique aspects (as independently elected bodies that express specific interests), is incompatible with the existence of a common Presidium superior to both Chambers, which would inevitably inhibit this independence and suppress these differences.

We recall, furthermore, that the Presidium of the Supreme Soviet is regarded as essentially a collective head of government. The election of the president makes this role of the Presidium of the Supreme Soviet unnecessary.

Finally, it is illustrative that there are no examples of such organs as the Presidium of the Supreme Soviet in the design or operation of bicameral parliaments in any democratic state in the world.

8.
FUNDAMENTAL JUDICIAL REFORM

The draft Constitution has significantly enhanced the judicial branch, as manifested primarily in an expansion of the legal protection of all rights and freedoms from possible assault from any quarter.

The Declaration of State Sovereignty of the RSFSR and the new Constitution lay the groundwork for the establishment in Russia of a self-sustaining, strong and independent judicial branch that has not previously existed in our country. The judicial system has been a continuation of the administrative-command system, operating as its servant by obsequiously executing the directives of the governing Party. The dependent courts lost the confidence of society, which justifiable perceived them to be simply the punitive organs of a totalitarian state.

Guided by the idea of a government of laws, the draft Constitution of the Russian Federation establishes the judicial branch by assigning to it the role of defender of civil peace and the rights and freedoms of man and citizen, and by imposing on it the obligation to guarantee legality and good will.

The judicial branch becomes the principal force in the system of organs for protection of rights, which is entirely under its control. The independence of judges is guaranteed by their immunity from discharge. The wholly-compromised courts of people's assessors are replaced by courts with juries: truly the people's courts. The restoration of justices of the peace elected by the people for review of administrative, civil rights, minor civil and, possibly, criminal matters, is envisaged.

The Supreme Court of the Russian Federation stands at the apex of the Federal judicial system.

The Constitutional Court of the Russian Federation is charged with conservation and observation of constitutional legality and is given broad powers of constitutional supervision over the activity of the legislative and executive branches.

The Procurator, now relieved of functions not suitable for this position in a government of laws, essentially becomes the government prosecutor and the professional director of investigations.

Investigations of criminal matters are transferred from the domain of the KGB, MVD and the procurators and are concentrated in a special state organ.

9.
LEGISLATIVE PROGRAM

1) Draft Constitution and Current Legislation

The new Constitution was not born in a vacuum. The basic provisions of a number of laws adopted by the Supreme Soviet of the RSFSR and the USSR were considered in drafting the Constitution.

They include specifically:
-the RSFSR law on property in the RSFSR;
-the RSFSR law on employment of the population;
-the RSFSR law on state pensions in the RSFSR
-the RSFSR law on states of emergency
-the RSFSR land code;
-the RSFSR law on peasant (farm) economy
-the RSFSR law on land reform
-the RSFSR law on labor unions, rights and guarantees of their activity;
-the RSFSR law on enterprises and entrepreneurial activity;
-the RSFSR law on competition and limited monopolistic activity in the trade markets;
-the RSFSR law on the President of the RSFSR;
-the RSFSR law on election of the President of the RSFSR;
-the regulations of the Supreme Soviet of the RSFSR
-the law on the status of a people's deputy of the RSFSR;
-the RSFSR law on the Constitutional Court of the RSFSR;
-the RSFSR law on the state tax service of the RSFSR;
-the law on banks and banking activity in the RSFSR;
-the RSFSR law on the militia [police];
-the RSFSR law on referenda;
-the RSFSR law on freedom of religion;
-the USSR law on citizenship;
-the USSR law on the general origins of local self government and local economy in the USSR;
-the USSR law on property in the USSR;
-the USSR law on pensions for military service personnel;

-the USSR law on pensions for citizens of the USSR;
-the USSR law on the legal state of emergency;
-the USSR law on enterprises in the USSR;
-the USSR law on the common origins of enterprise by citizens in the USSR;
-the USSR law on protection of consumers' rights;
-the USSR law on social associations;
-the USSR law on free national development of citizens of the USSR living outside of their national-state formations or having no such citizenship on the territory of the USSR;
-the USSR law on the press and other mass media;
-the USSR law on the procedure for solving problems relating to the secession of a union republic from the USSR;
-the USSR law on the principles of economic relationships of the USSR, the union and autonomous republics;
-the USSR law on the delineation of authority between the USSR and subjects of the Federation;
-the USSR law on institution of the position of President of the USSR and amendments and supplements to the constitution (primary law) of the USSR;
-the USSR law on the status of a people's deputy of the USSR;
-the USSR law on the procedure for recalling people's deputies of the USSR
-the USSR law on the Cabinet of Ministers of the USSR;
-the USSR law on constitutional supervision in the USSR;
-the USSR law on banks and banking activity;
-the USSR law on the Soviet militia;
-the USSR law on organs of state security of the USSR;
-the USSR law on referenda;
-the USSR law on freedom of conscience and religious organizations;
-the USSR law on the languages of the peoples of the USSR

2) Legislative Program.

Likewise the Constitution does not represent the end of a certain path and set the final result in concrete; it rather outlines directions for the development of the state and opens the doors to new reforms in various areas of the life of man.

The draft Constitution provides a clear plan for the upcoming legislative activity of the Supreme Council by providing a constitutional basis for transformations made and contemplated. The draft Constitution contains references to numerous laws. They will reveal the status of the new

Constitution and supplement the constitutional reform with a package of coordinated, specific reforms that cover: administrative-territorial subdivisions, state organs, agrarian, military, legal, local self government, etc.

These laws are an extension of the constitution. The parliament is to focus on the adoption of such laws in the near future. Below is a general list of the required acts:

Law on the electoral system
Law on preservation of individual rights (including the right of free movement)
Law on state secrets
Law on citizenship
Law on local self government
Law on the procedure for resolving personal appeals by citizens
Law on the status of the Russian Federation Commissioner for Human Rights
Law on taxation of citizens
Law on land and land use
Law on social security
Law on the criminal procedure code
Law on the profession of the law
Law on states of emergency
Law on military service and alternative civilian service
Law on unions
Law on entrepreneurial activity
Law on resolution of labor disputes (strikes)
Law on political parties
Law on the status and borders of the republics (or lands)
Law on the procedure for forming new lands in the territory of existing republics and lands
Law on the President
Law on Regulations of the Chambers of the Supreme Council
Law on government service
Law on the judicial system
Law on the Supreme Council of the Russian Federation
Law on the Security Council of the Russian Federation
Law on the Council of Ministers of the Russian Federation
Law on The Constitutional Court of the Russian Federation
Law on procurators
Law on the Committee of Inquiry
Law on the budget system

Law on the armed forces
Law on the Federal Security Service
Law on the State Coat of Arms
Law on the State Hymn
Law on the State Flag
Law on the Service of the President of the Russian Federation
Law on the State Treasury

APPENDIX 2

EXPLANATION OF CERTAIN TERMS USED IN THE DRAFT OF THE CONSTITUTION OF THE RUSSIAN FEDERATION

The State Treasury of the Russian Federation is an organ created by the Supreme Council of the Russian Federation to monitor the preparation, consideration, adoption, implementation and reporting on implementation of the budget of the Russian Federation (the Federal budget) and the expenditure of budgeted allocations by state organs and institutions.

State Sovereignty is the supremacy of a given government within its own territory and its independence in international affairs. A government with state sovereignty in a certain territory excludes the possibility that another sovereign government may be in power in that same territory. In appropriate cases, both with respect to domestic and to foreign affairs, unilateral or mutual delegation (transfer) of authority, of jurisdiction, etc., is permitted, although this does not constitute a ceding or reduction of sovereignty within the territory.

International agreements to which the Russian Federation is a party. In accordance with the Vienna Convention on the rights in international agreements to which the USSR is a party, the law of the USSR "On the Procedure for Ratification, Execution and Denunciation of International Agreements of the USSR" of 1988, uses a common term to represent the names of various international legal acts of a formal nature -- international agreements, pacts, memoranda, regulations, charters, etc.: the term "international agreement."

Since any agreement between constituent republics of the USSR is based on said republics operating as sovereign states, such inter-republic agreements are consistent with the "international agreement" classification.

The people -- all the citizens of the Russian Federation (this state) the republics and lands, regardless of their national affiliation. The use of this constitutional concept in no way prevents the recognition or guarantee in a republic or land of the right to autonomy for individual regions or nationalities.

Generally recognized principles and norms of international law -- legal principles and norms acknowledged by virtually all states as commonly binding in international affairs and for implementation on their own territories with respect to their own citizens.

Public Associations -- political parties, labor unions, public organizations, mass movements, religious and other public associations which do not have as their purpose a profit motive.

Principles of the constitutional structure of the Russian Federation -- the founding, fundamental legal principles and norms, defining the main, essential characteristics of the Russian Federation, the basic features of its structure, the general content of the Constitution, the general prospects for legislation, the framework of law and other legal acts.

Primary territorial collectives of public self government -- collectives that may be formed by residents of populated regions that are not territorial units, into which the republics and lands are divided. They undertake public self government, independent of the state government of the Russian Federation, the governments of the republics or lands local self government.

Preamble -- the introductory portion of a document, having the same legal force as the other parts of the document.

Direct action of Constitutional standards -- the direct obligation created by constitutional standards, requiring no confirmation or specifying standards, laws or other legal acts, but not excluding the possibility of the adoption of such acts and laws in cases specifically stated in the Constitution, as well as other expedient cases.

Public property -- the property of the Russian Federation (state property), the property of the republics, lands, the property of self governing territorial associations, the property of primary territorial collectives of public self government, the property of public associations.

Entrepreneurial associations -- economic units (corporations, societies with limited liability, etc.) and other such entrepreneurial subjects that have a profit motive as the reason for their activity.

Self governing territorial associations -- associations of persons, whose primary purpose of association is territorial association. They exist only in territorial units into which the republics and lands are divided, and encompass the entire territory of a unit. They administer local self government and are independent of the state government of the Russian Federation and the government of the republic or land.

Commissioner of the Russian Federation for Human Rights -- the person who supervises the observation within the Russian Federation, the republics and lands and self governing territorial associations the rights and freedoms of man and citizen. He acts directly and through his territorial representatives. He does not replace or preclude the actions of other state organs devoted to the supervision and protection of these rights and freedoms. The republics and lands may also create their own commissioners of human rights or other organs with the same tasks.

The institution of the commissioner for human rights is widely known in World constitutional practice and is active in Great Britain, Poland, Spain and many other countries.

Federal law -- a law of the Russian Federation, adopted by the Supreme Council of the Russian Federation, in contrast to laws adopted by the republics and lands. It is enforced throughout the territory of the Russian Federation, in contrast to the laws of the republics and lands, which are enforced only on the territory of the corresponding republic or land.

Private property -- property of individual persons and property of enterprise associations.

APPENDIX 3

WORKING GROUP OF THE CONSTITUTIONAL COMMISSION OF THE RSFSR

***NOTE:** This dictionary will be expanded.

The draft was prepared by a working group, consisting of:
People's deputies of the RSFSR -- F.M. Adrov, Ye.A. Ambartsumov, F.Sh. Arslanova, L.B. Volkiov, B.A. Zolotukhin, S.A. Kovalev, P.A. Medvedev, R.I. Pimenov, O.G. Rumyantsev (group leader), Yu.A. Ryzhov, S.M. Sirotkin, F.V. Tsann-Kay-Si, V.L. Sheynis, F.V. Shelov-Kovedyayev, and also A.M. Obolenskiy (people's deputy of the USR).

Consultants -- F.E. Zor'kin, V.A. Kikot', L.S. Mamut, B.A. Strashun, and also E.M. Ametistov, Ye.A. Danilov, T.G. Morshakova, M.P. Petrosyan, B.M. Pugachev, M.V. Odintsov.

The leader of the secretariat of the Commission was A.A. Goltsblat.

The work on the draft Constitution of the Russian Federation involved the members of the Constitutional Commission of the RSFSR, as well as people's deputies of the RSFSR, USSR, the Moscow City Council and the Moscow Oblast Council. Comments and suggestions of the committees and commissions of the Supreme Soviet of the RSFSR, groups of specialists of the RSFSR Ministry of Justice, a number of research institutes and law schools, as well as individual social scientists, were considered. Foreign experts also provided comments and suggestions.

SUBJECT INDEX